GOING FORE IT
in golf & life

Angelo,

Distance off the
tee is infinite

"Go fore it"

with passion

[signature]

GOING FORE IT
in golf & life

gil anderson

iUniverse, Inc.
Bloomington

Going Fore It
In Golf and Life

iUniverse books may be ordered through booksellers or by contacting:

iUniverse
1663 Liberty Drive
Bloomington, IN 47403
www.iuniverse.com
1-800-Authors (1-800-288-4677)

*Because of the dynamic nature of the Internet, any Web addresses or links contained in this book
may have changed since publication and may no longer be valid.*

*Any people depicted in stock imagery provided by Thinkstock are models,
and such images are being used for illustrative purposes only.*

Certain stock imagery © Thinkstock.

ISBN: 978-1-4502-8682-4 (sc)
ISBN: 978-1-4502-8684-8 (dj)
ISBN: 978-1-4502-8683-1 (ebk)

Library of Congress Control Number: 2011901497

Printed in the United States of America

iUniverse rev. date: 2/8/2011

To my wife, Beth —

Our many days on the golf course have been the inspiration for the thoughts that began this journey, but it was your love and support that always gave me the courage to see this project to completion. You have made both this work and my life complete.

Contents

Foreword

The Nature of the Game

Allow me to introduce myself. I am the game of golf. I have a long and honored history and tradition. My origins may be traced back as far as the early days of the Roman Empire as a game called Paganica, played with bent sticks and a leather ball stuffed with feathers. I evolved from there into what I am today, highly technical, with equipment designed through advanced technology, in an effort to dominate my elusive, mystical nature. Regardless of these efforts, I always remain one up on even my most capable of participants. Even with their gyroscopic, elliptical balanced, optimized pendulum putters they still miss their three foot putts. At those moments, I take pride in the control that I have over their doubting minds.

I am most proud of my formal association with the Royal and Ancient Golf Club of St. Andrews, Scotland, founded in 1754. My history is extensive and should be infused in all who become acquainted. I am a game of integrity and honesty instilled in all who play, carried out with pride and dignity from the depths of the divine nature of their being. I maintain a capacity to affect the human condition in a profound way, connecting the inner workings of the body, mind, and spirit in an interaction with a fundamental value system that reflects the ideals that I have always maintained. I promise to provide for all who wish to play the best that I have to give, but I expect the same in return.

I require the highest respect for the beauty and tranquility of the environments which have been laid out for play. I invite you to accept and be grateful for the challenges provided by the creative minds of designers of the most difficult courses, while at the same time appreciate the simplest of course designs. Regardless of where you play, it is my greatest pleasure to deliver to you those special, joyful moments of exhilaration. These connect you with that wonderful feeling of an effortless ball strike as you bear witness to the aesthetic beauty of its soaring flight against a clear, blue sky. For it will be in the poetry of that moment that your spirit will be lifted with the soaring flight of the ball.

Be advised that I require commitment and strength of character, as no one has ever mastered my unique nature. You must indulge yourself wholeheartedly in me, but let your game develop at its own pace. Do not compare yourself to others. Maintain humility in your victories; never be boastful for I will descend upon you with great vengeance. Be encouraging to others who may be experiencing difficulty. Cherish your search for an individual understanding of my being and appreciate your strengths without ego. Work diligently on your weaknesses as you discover the untapped abilities that still lie dormant within you. My spirit requires great tenacity and strength of character for there can be no master of my nature. I require an intuitive connection, combined with an intellectual, rational mind-set. I will not tolerate any outward release of frustration or exhibition of improper conduct, whether it is verbal or physical. It detracts from the dignity I represent. You will only bring upon yourself a negative response, reflecting on your character, but also negatively affecting the attitudes of those around you. Remain a dignified role model and I will reward you with good fortune.

Seek advice when it is needed from instructors that go beyond the simple mechanics of the game. Allow them to tap into the depths of your being and release a true understanding as they inspire and motivate you. Allow them to affect the childlike enthusiasm necessary to truly connect with what I offer you.

Commit yourself to maintaining physical well-being. The human body in its intricate design deserves your commitment to maintain it at the highest level of efficiency. God perfectly designed the human mind, body, and spirit to respond effortlessly to my demands. Cherish what you have been provided with. Nourish yourself by connecting with the pursuit of my challenge as it encourages you to attend to your physical, mental, and spiritual development. With proper, focused attention, you have an opportunity to enjoy blissful days on the rolling fairways and smooth, undulating greens for the rest of your life.

It now gives me great pleasure to introduce you to one of my most devoted disciples. At an early age, he became interested in my nature and has continued his commitment to my life's lessons through his playing and teaching. Through him I am able to communicate my purpose. His name is Gil Anderson. He is the author of this book, which I have entrusted in his care. He leaves this book as a permanent legacy of what I have had the joy of sharing with him. In the following pages he picks up my message and shares it with you. My wish is that you will instill within yourself the passion, the purpose, the process, and the pursuit of all that you aspire to. With patience and perseverance, I will always be with you on the playing course of your future in golf and life.

Introduction

After many years of consideration, I have finally decided that it is time to share what I have learned from a passionate relationship with golf. Throughout my life, I have enjoyed the privilege of studying and playing this most incredible game. I have been led through divine guidance to opportunities that allow me to share my ever-expanding knowledge as a teacher. This has provided me with a motivational force that has had a profound effect on all aspects of my life. It is now my commitment to share my reflections on golf and its relationship to a life force that has inspired a growing realization of who I am and what I stand for.

As I sit in contemplation of the many years of experiences, I think back to the people, the places, and the events that have passed through my life and my dedication to the game. But, as I begin my recollections and work on sorting out what *it* is that is important to share, I can't help but think of what qualifies me to put another book about the game of golf on the shelves. What is it about the game that deserves more documented evidence of its very existence? I suppose part of my purpose is the simple reminiscence of years gone by and those miraculous moments on the many golf courses that I have had the pleasure of playing. Those memories flood back into my mind as if it were yesterday, along with the playing partners whose time shared was a great privilege.

Through my experiences, without my knowing, I was destined to become a teacher of the game. It was never a direct intent, but as this career as a golf instructor developed, I realized that there was always a situation or circumstance that drew me to the profession. I never pursued this on a full time basis. It was always necessary to maintain a real job to support myself and my family. However, seasonal work was always available so I could share my knowledge and experience over the last thirty-seven years. My students have been my inspiration. They continue to energize me as I have the privilege of witnessing their growth and childlike enthusiasm as they unlock their inner ability to strike a golf ball. Simple as it may seem, first solid contact remains a magical event. At that moment, my students and I have joined in a kinship of understanding that defies logic, as it taps into a spiritual connection with the divinity of the game. Now, at my present age, I am getting close, not to retirement, but rather to a freedom to pursue a fulltime dedication to do my part in the continuing growth of the game. At this point in my life, I have made a dramatic commitment to achieving optimal health and wellness that allows me to contemplate the next two or three decades of sharing my knowledge and passion.

I would like to acknowledge a number of people along the way that have had an instrumental effect in my development. First and foremost, my thanks go to my father, even though he never had the opportunity or desire to play the game he ignited the spark within me. Initially, my curiosity for the game came from an episode of the *I Love Lucy* television show, featuring the game in a typical Lucy/Desi fashion. This inspired my desire to ask my Dad for his assistance in getting me started. My father told me that it was not likely that I would ever become a golfer because it was a "rich man's game." Despite this, he was kind enough to bring home a ladies brassie. He cut down the club to properly fit my six year old body and wrapped the wooden shaft with electrical tape to prevent splinters. Dad then bought me a dozen wiffle golf balls, and sent me out into the yard to play. That's all it took–I was hooked! That one club led to the addition of a niblick, a mashie, and a putter which completed my entire first set of clubs. Dad then built a putting green for me in our back yard where I would spend my endless summer days playing the golf course that I had laid out around my house. That course served as my early training ground.

Dow Finsterwald, a famous golf pro at the time, had a fifteen minute golf show on television called *Golf Tip of the Day*. It ran a number of times and featured different aspects of the game. I would make sure not to miss a single episode and then would run back out into the yard to put into practice what I had learned. Thank you, Dow, for being my first instructor. I still teach many of his techniques today. "Andersonville Country Club" remained my course of choice until I was eleven years old.

We moved a short distance from Hartsdale to White Plains, New York, temporarily breaking my heart. By this time I had a full set of clubs and my Dad was taking me to the driving range where I developed a reasonable ability to play. He would look on with great pride as other people at the range would notice my ability and my desire. These people asked in an admiring way, "Is that **your** son?" With great pride he looked on and nodded. From there, we progressed to Maple Moor, the local public golf course, where Dad convinced the pro that I was more than capable to play along with any group of people. The pro checked me out and quickly agreed. Dad would drop me off in the morning with a bag lunch and a dollar seventy-five for my greens fee. By the end of the first month, I had steady playing partners who would ask for my advice. Alas, my first introduction to teaching. I loved every minute of it. Soon, I picked up an afternoon group as well who were more than happy to pay my greens fees and buy my lunch. My parents never knew that I was playing thirty-six holes a day, pocketing my dollar seventy-five, and trashing my bag lunch. The experience from age eleven to fourteen set the stage for my future with the game. Thank you, Dad; I would have had a very different life without you.

By the time I was fourteen, I met some older friends who convinced me to start caddying just up the road from Maple Moor at Westchester Country Club. Westchester was a great training ground for analyzing golf swings. My observations became very helpful in my ability to evaluate results. Westchester Country Club was also very liberal in providing playing privileges for their loyal caddies. I won the caddie championship a number of years in a row, which was a great boast to my less than confident nature. Thank you, Westchester Country Club for my memories from the caddy shack.

During these years, I played on the varsity golf team at White Plains High School. This proved to be a great experience, although I was the only player whose parents were not country club members. The acceptance of my lower social status, however, provided me with a tremendous opportunity to develop more self-assuredness. The golf coach at that time, Mr. Clegg, took a special liking to me. I think he admired my tenacity and the respect that I had for the game, as well as the appreciation that I had for his time and attention. I still remember his last words to me at our final high school match. I had just sunk a thirty-five foot, double breaking putt on the last green, which led to our final win. He said, "It has been my great pleasure knowing you. This game will take you far and provide you with what you need in life." I wasn't sure what he meant by that, but now, after all these years of involvement, I understand his meaning. Thank you, Mr. Clegg.

Following graduation from high school, I went on to play varsity golf at Westchester Community College. Those times were very interesting and stressful due to the military draft. It was the height of the Vietnam War and the final destination for many of my fellow male graduates. My attitude toward my studies was quite pitiful. At that time, I believe that it was only the game of golf that kept me on the straight and narrow path.

A year and a half after high school, I left college, was drafted into the Marine Corps, but was able to quickly enlist in the Air Force. Due to some natural talent in art, my duty assignment was as an illustrator, fundamentally working as a commercial artist. This position was a fortunate blessing. I had a lot of freedom, was quite adept at my work, and was very much appreciated for my talent. The best part was yet to come. It seemed that to my surprise, Barksdale Air Force Base in Shreveport, Louisiana, where I was first stationed, had one of the best golf courses in the entire Air Force. When the officers in my squadron discovered my ability to play and teach the game of golf, my future days were filled with wonderful opportunities to play competitive golf and share my knowledge of the game with the upper echelon of both officers and visiting dignitaries. I would have to thank God for that good fortune. Once again golf came to my rescue and kept me out of harm's way.

After being discharged from the Air Force, I returned to Westchester Community College to complete my associate degree. This time I took my studies very seriously, eventually transferring and graduating with honors from the State University at New Paltz. It was at Westchester, however, that I found the greatest gift in my life. I met my soul mate, Beth and proposed to her on our very first date. By some miracle she accepted. This event was undoubtedly the best thing that **ever** happened in my life.

So after graduating from Westchester, off we went to New Paltz, not knowing how we were ever going to be able to survive. Within one year, we had our only child, Melanie. We did not know how we were ever going to make our way in the world. That first summer I needed a job, so after settling the three of us into our little studio apartment, I set out in search of any employment that would be compatible with my educational responsibilities. As I drove just a short way up the road, I came upon a sign that read Locust Tree Golf and Country Club. I am not sure what happened, but my car made a hard left hand turn down that driveway! At the end of the road, the parking area opened up to a beautiful, newly constructed golf course. As I got out of the car, the superintendent greeted me and, after a short chat, asked me if I had my clubs with me. I told him that I never left home without them. His name was Ray Frisch and he invited me to play a round of golf, on him. I accepted, we proceeded to the first tee, and he watched me tee off on that par 5 hole. I cracked a good drive down the middle of the fairway followed by a second shot around the corner setting up a birdie on the first hole. I was in my glory. I understood because of my meager finances that this would probably be the only round of golf I would be able to play until I finished college. I made the best of it though, and had a reasonable two over par round, recording a birdie on the last hole. Ray was on the back porch of the pro shop and I went up to thank him again. As we talked, he asked me if I always played golf that well. I explained that I had not been playing that much lately, but maintained a low handicap when I had the time to play and practice. The next words out of his mouth were truly a gift from the Golf Gods. He asked me if I would like a job as a golf pro. I was stunned, but told him that I was not a pro. He simply replied with, "Well, would you like to be?" I immediately accepted and made a commitment to *go fore it*.

I had to explain my situation, though. How would I attend college and cover my responsibilities as a golf pro? He told me that they could hire someone to cover the shop while I was in class. I quickly interrupted with, "I have just the person for the job, my wife, Beth." Ray and I set a time for me to meet with the decision making owner, George Mackey, and I returned home. Upon arriving, I was so excited I could hardly express myself. Beth greeted me at the door and noticed that I had a little sunburn on my face. She wondered where I had been searching for employment. As I told her about discovering a golf course she interrupted with, "I thought you were out looking for a job?" My immediate response was, "Don't worry, I got *us* a job!" Beth's retort was, "What do you mean *us*?" The rest is history. My thanks go out to George Mackey and Ray Frisch, who saw something in me and set me on a more formal path of teaching and performing the duties of a golf pro.

Golf again came to my rescue and helped get us through the next years of school. After graduating from New Paltz with a degree in art education, I secured a teaching job in the Taconic Hills School District in Hillsdale, New York. During my first year, one of my students, John Shakshober, had heard that I was a golf professional and informed me that his father was building a golf course on their property in Boston Corner. He kindly invited me down to the course for a round of golf. The next thing I knew, I once again had a job as a golf pro, this time at Undermountain Golf Course. I was provided with an excellent summer position that complemented my work as a public school teacher. During those days, my wife, Beth, began to play and developed an interest in the game. She quickly became my favorite golfing partner, especially as her golf game improved over the years. We have enjoyed sharing many memorable days of golf and look forward to many more. Once again, the game of golf provided me with what I needed to satisfy my efforts and also the financial assistance necessary to supplement my teaching salary. Many thanks go out to the Shakshober family, Jack and Pat, their sons, Stuart and John (DJ) and their daughter, Trish. My memories of our time together will always hold a fond place in my heart.

Through a series of circumstances, I changed careers and began working as a financial consultant. This required us to move from the Berkshire Mountain Region of New York down to the Hudson River area in Orange County. During this time, the game of golf became even more important than ever. I discovered the power the game had in networking with other professionals, which opened up many business opportunities. After settling down in Montgomery, New York, Beth and I joined Otterkill Country Club. After a short time, I found myself back on the practice tee working as an assistant teaching professional. I would like to thank John Schmoll, the head golf pro for that opportunity. After a few delightful years teaching there, I was offered my present position at Winding Hills Golf Course, right in my hometown of Montgomery.

This current position is quite unique and is a perfect fit for me at this time in my life. Golf is now a passionate involvement as I share much of who I am, while I help my students have a recreational experience that transcends the mere mechanics of the game. Winding Hills is an executive length golf course that has been designed to meticulous perfection. Due to its exquisitely intricate design, it presents all the difficulties of some of the more challenging of layouts, but still offers the beginner an opportunity to play. The lavish flower gardens, surrounded by the carefully designed clubhouse, restaurant, and adjoining patio add to the aesthetic consciousness. This provides a relaxing, restorative environment for socialization. The staff has been well-trained to treat every person as a special guest. The entire experience at Winding Hills is a model for the commitment to excellence to which my own life has been dedicated. I have had the privilege of focusing one hundred percent of my efforts on teaching without interference in my methods. This freedom has enabled me to discover a great deal of insight into how the human psyche effects and interconnects with bodily movement. This in turn has opened the door to a whole new awareness of how the game of golf needs to be taught and learned. The results that I have witnessed over the past seven years have been quite profound. My instructional lessons have been continuously expanded in their content as I have realized so much more about this magical game and its relationship to life.

For my present position, I must give thanks to the Devitt family, particularly Ed and Marc, for their commitment to growing an interest in golf in the community through the gift of Winding Hills Golf Course. My personal gratitude goes to all of the Devitts for the support and belief that they have entrusted in me. This is a family that truly understands the spirit behind the purpose of this book. I look forward to a long tenure as their golf professional.

My greatest thanks go out to my wife, Beth. She is my soul mate and my reason for life and living. Without her I would not have had the unfailing support and encouragement necessary to continue my inquisitive search into new methods of communicating the nature of this cherished game. To you, Beth, I dedicated the writing of this book. You have empowered me to *go fore it*.

Finally, I would like to thank the many thousands of students of all ages, physical abilities, and reasons for playing. I would like to think that I have taught something more than just game of golf. I hope I have touched your lives and positively affected your individual life force.

In the following pages, I will clarify what my life in golf has given me and share the life lessons that I have graciously accepted. I hope to leave it as an inspiring legacy to the many people who have helped me along the way as my passion, my purpose, my process, and my pursuit continues to evolve with patience, and perseverance.

Part One

The Passion

Passion is a powerful aspect of human nature. It is a force that brings forth the motivation that effectively enables a connection with any desired accomplishment. As long as the heartfelt passion endures, even the most difficult of endeavors can be conquered. At many times I ask myself, what is it about the game that not only has kept my interest over so many years, but continues to tantalize my imagination. What inspires a desire to delve into the deeper meaning that exists within the heart of the game? There seems to be something more to *it* than what lies on the surface of birdies, pars, and bogies.

In Chapter One, we examine the *it factor* of the game. There is a spiritual aspect of connectedness that is extremely alluring. If we allow ourselves the privilege of total engagement, we are able to truly connect to what *it* is about golf. Chapter Two reveals the insight of how and why it is so important to maintain our passion if we are to achieve a satisfying involvement in our efforts. We discover that the game of golf has something within *it* that brings us to a higher ground of self-realization. As we move on to Chapter Three, our individual character is discovered as we examine what it is within us that creates and supports our passionate commitment. We begin our examination and consideration through the fulfillment of our desire, which lies within the cornerstone of our passion. Chapter Four sets us on a quest for the secret within the discovery of how we play our game in life. As the secret unfolds, we are able to come closer to a depth of holistic consciousness that further reveals the *it factor* of the game. Finally, in Chapter Five, we realize the connection through the infinite nature that resides within the eternal spirit flowing through all things. In this chapter, we learn how to activate and accept the importance of our Karma and Dharma, as we penetrate the inner mind game and explore the outer limits of our potential. Now, I invite you to join me as we begin our journey to release the power that lies within the passion for the game.

The effect on our human condition can be influenced in a grand manner as we continue our search, always hoping to uncover the inner secrets held in the playing fields of our lives.

Chapter One

It's a Game! It's Only a Game! Or is it?

The *It Factor*

So what is *it* about the game of golf that has inspired so many people of all ages, abilities, walks of life, and nationalities to find a common ground in a kindred spirit of oneness? The search for meaning of *it* has produced an evolution in all aspects of the game. Club design has undergone intense research and development, utilizing space age technology. Advanced materials in metallurgy have been on the cutting edge of research while balancing the development between the striking surfaces and weighing systems. As studies delve further into shaft designs with fluctuating flex points, the steel and graphite components produce varying ball flights, initial velocity, and spin ratios. These developments increased both distance and accuracy. Our passion for perfection has overcome us. Even the golf balls have evolved. At one time they were constructed using hand sewn, leather covers that were stuffed with feathers resembling small baseballs. Now, they have gone through an innovative advancement, making their various core structures and dimple patterns more aerodynamic. Presently, we have a ball for every swing speed and launch angle, yet the mastery of the game still remains elusive while the game remains the same.

To counteract this advancement in technology the new breed of course designers, including some of the top players, progressively configure their creations with a higher level of difficulty. Their expectations hope to offset the increased performance of the equipment. What kind of insanity is this that they would go to these lengths all in the name of golf? It supports a passion in the spirit of all who love the challenge of the game.

Yet, it's not all of these advancements and involvement that truly lie at the core of the *it factor* of the game. There seems to be something more that penetrates to the core of the human need to satisfy the mind, body, and spirit. As we continue to search for *it* we get ever closer, but in a fleeting moment *it* escapes us in *its* elusive manner. Once again we continue our self-imposed task to capture *it*.

I think of so many times in my own playing and teaching that I truly feel that "Oh, I've got it now." Or I've heard one of my students remark "I've finally got it!" Inevitably they return for their lesson to show me their cherished accomplishment, only to fail miserably, and comment that now "They've lost it." We are all feeble in our thinking to believe that we can ever come to a full understanding of why we cannot master the requirements of the game.

Ask yourself, "Why should I continue this futile effort?" We don't throw our clubs in the pond, walk away from the game, or even hang our head in shame and disgust. Instead, we continue to try to find something in *it,* however *it* always seems to remain just outside our grasp. Spurred on by our passion, we continue our efforts hoping for the next magical moment of a chip in, a long breaking putt that drops in the hole on its last revolution or perhaps even a miraculous hole-in-one. At these times our human spirit is lifted to heights beyond comprehension and we are reminded why we play. We are moving ever closer to the nature of *it*.

Pain and Pleasure

Human motivation for learning must have at its root a passionate need to truly want something so badly that the spirit will endure and overcome any difficulty that blocks its realization. At the core of our experience, lies the basic force of our sensibility. These are simply the aspects of pain and pleasure. The question is will we do more to avoid pain than we will to seek pleasure?

There is no getting around one simple understanding that golf requires practice. I have often heard it said by many of my students that they love to play, but hate to practice. There can be so much more pleasure derived from playing if we can find effective, economical ways to practice. This is one of the reasons that I recommend that my students practice with wiffle balls. Now they can have the convenience of utilizing their back yard as a driving range. There is no need to set aside a significant amount of time. Fifteen minutes, including the travel time spent going to the back yard once a day can produce great pleasure on the golf course. So, if we can find ways to remove the pain from practice, we have cleared the way to allow our passion to be fully realized in a much greater pleasure.

Chipping and pitching can be easily accomplished with regulation golf balls in the yard. This part of the game is all about feel. If you put in the time to make repetitions of stroke and contact, your confidence grows quickly and releases the passionate feelings that you have as you look forward to your next day on the course. I encourage you to fall in love with your practice sessions.

Putting should not be neglected either. This can be practiced inside on a smooth carpet. If you want to get more elaborate, you can purchase a putting mat, many of which have automatic ball returns. Time spent working on a smooth stroke is one of the best ways to avoid pain and seek pleasure. This is particularly true from within three feet. Challenge yourself to release the passionate putter inside you and feel the childlike enthusiasm arise from within, as you realize that this is more than just a game.

As we continue to satisfy the passion within us, we begin to realize how the game can have a profound effect on our very existence. Our willingness is released from our desire to force results. This in turn energizes and enables us to unlock a new found work ethic that is not burdensome, but rather flows from the power of an inner force. This gives us endless, effortless endurance to experience without any attachment to the outcome. We learn to let it happen rather than forcing on the game a willful desire to control. Our aspirations are fully realized as we become one with the game. The effect on our human condition can be influenced in a grand manner as we continue our search, always hoping to uncover the inner secrets held in the playing fields of our lives.

Passionate Play

We can be transformed only if we allow ourselves the unrestricted release of our passion which provides a gift to the human spirit. Through experience, we play in all aspects of our lives, releasing unrestricted enthusiasm. It is passion that reveals our true inner self along with the authentic nature of our being. Passionate involvement allows us to live our lives to the fullest and move past the restrictions of caution, often holding us back.

Ask yourself the question, "How would I play the shot if I knew I couldn't fail?" You could then take the leap of faith and seek your highest, joyful experience. If we are willing to take that risk, passion can ignite explosive inspiration and creativity revealing our unrealized abilities. This, in turn, supports the purpose and mission in our pursuit of play. Should you try that impossible golf shot and fail, you are at least stretching yourself to the next level. But, should you succeed, you release an adrenaline rush that allows the human spirit to soar and move ever closer to the heart of the game. This willingness is what I refer to as "perfect play." It is not defined by the score that you record. Perfect play is not about winning or losing. It is about how you participate in the game. Passion for practice and play increases your desire. With ever growing commitment, your tenacity will grow to levels that overcome any obstacle. This, in turn, leads to higher levels of accomplishment and capacity. Self-esteem will soar, allowing determination and belief to overcome the pain of pursuit. The passion continues to grow as your belief leads to self-reliance moving ever closer to a connection to the *it* factor of the game.

The Playground of Passion

As you continue to experience the growth in your understanding of the physical aspects of the game, such as body mechanics and techniques of ball striking, allow yourself to also be immersed in the beauty and tranquility of the surroundings of the golf course. The course architect, along with the grounds superintendent, have miraculously designed and manicured each subtle detail for your enjoyment.

Each spring, when my wife and I return to the course, we have the joy of witnessing the rebirth of the surroundings. As we begin our golfing year here in the Northeast, the environment is grey and brown. Only tinges of the emerald green of what will be the lush turf of the near future are peering through, surviving the harsh winter. The chill winds of winter whistle through the barren trees reminding us of the passing of the season, but they cannot maintain their hold on our anticipation of what is soon to come. The first warm day finally arrives with penetrating rays of sun melting away the last of the morning frost. Once again our addiction for the game is rekindled. We are sure that this will be the best golfing year of our lives. Practice sessions now restore our faith. As we strike the first ball of the year, the belief is renewed in our potential. Reassurance that we have not forgotten how to play over the long winter is once again re-established connecting with our dormant golfing spirit. Another season has finally arrived.

Now, as the spring progresses and the sun's rays become more direct, we notice the budding trees. Day by day, they continue to unfold, resurrecting the beauty of the lined fairways with their lurking overhanging limbs that seem to reach out to challenge our abilities. The trees are a miracle as they provide a scale of size for us to understand the relativity of distance and height. We gaze across the tree line for a moment, as our ball seems to hover in endless flight. We are fully alive again and our hearts are lifted with a passionate resurgence of desire.

With spring's emergence wildlife again abounds on the golf course. Each year we have the privilege to witness the renewal of so many species. First, we observe the return of the geese and we patiently wait for the birth of this year's families. Although these birds are sometimes not looked upon fondly, especially on golf courses, we recognize and appreciate their place on Earth. As the first of the little "fuzz balls" appear, faithfully following mama and papa, we look forward to watching their maturation. We marvel at the swimming and the eventual flying lessons until finally, the day in late fall arrives when they begin their long flight south. Each species possesses its own evolving, magical show. The tadpoles to frogs, the first robins, and mama snapping turtle slowly making her trek in an unyielding determination to return to the same location to lay this year's eggs. These are the experiences that are associated with our own renewal of passion for the upcoming season. We are inspired by nature and its renewed surroundings. Like the first appearance of the season's fireflies, our determination and tenacity that often flicker and disappear have been rekindled. Our passion for the game and for life itself is renewed.

If we allow ourselves to become totally immersed in all aspects of the game, we realize a more holistic connection with all that is golf. Once again we recognize more of the intrinsic nature of its totality. It is truly more than just a game.

I would be remiss if I didn't recognize the dedication and hard work of the maintenance crew, spearheaded by the expertise of the course superintendent. I am always inspired by their passion for perfection. Awestruck, as I stand on the perfectly groomed tee, my eye glances down the fairway, captivated by the beautiful, rhythmic pattern of the fairway mower impressions that gracefully flow over the undulating terrain. This well-defined aesthetic beckons a desire for solid contact that sends my tee shot flying long and straight, settling on the perfectly manicured turf. Left and right of the fairway lie two meticulously raked bunkers, framing out the landing area as if they were surrounding a treasured painting, all while warning of the danger that lurks in their grasp. Their beautiful white sand, contrasted by the dark green fairway and rough, begins to play on our indecisiveness. Our spirit can now respond in successful, congruent flow of the well-timed swing or can fold to the doubts set up in our minds. As we try to over-control our efforts and end up in one of the sandy obstacles so devilishly placed, I often wonder if the maintenance staff derives a certain delight as they contemplate the affect that it has on the player.

As we continue approaching the green, we notice the greenskeeper just finished the morning cut as he examines the turf for any signs of insects or disease. Always, he is concerned for the smoothness and quality of the surface. On this particular imaginative moment, I notice that the flag and cup has been moved to a position that tempts proficiency of execution while presenting the possibility of total disaster. Once again, we may notice the sly smile on the turf master's face as he watches our efforts with anticipation. He remains equally satisfied, however, regardless of the outcome of our efforts.

Yes, we owe much of our continued passion for our pursuit to the tireless work of these dedicated professionals. I always take the time to thank them for their efforts and praise them for what they have given us as players of the game. Again, I realize that this is so much more than just a game— lending understanding of what *it* is all about.

Nineteenth Hole

At the end of each day, which is filled with many moments of exhilaration as well as frustration, I take time to marvel at what a unique experience it has been, different than any other. The interaction with our playing partners often carriers over for a little nourishment and a favorite beverage at the club's bar and restaurant. The camaraderie developed through the game should not be ignored; it's an important part of keeping the passion alive. Our support systems, constructed of likeminded people, provide a marvelous connection allowing us to share our day's disappointments and our future hopes and goals. Our desire to practice and play is renewed. Conversations are always lively, poking fun at one another, but never in a way that is not supportive to the spirit of golf. Jokes are shared, most of which we have heard before. We listen patiently and laugh appropriately in approval at each conclusion as if hearing it for the first time. It is all part of the subculture of the species we call golfing buddies. Now the conversation turns to a desire to share our golfing experiences of the past, the rounds we have played on great courses, and the people we have met. As we have these conversations our passion radiates. As we hear some of these same stories told again and again we realize the growth of exaggeration and challenge each other on the truthfulness of the related incidents being shared. Our passionate and exaggerated stories are necessary expressions of grandeur. They both support and motivate us to achieve and realize higher ability levels. So, we continue to allow ourselves to indulge in these casual meetings of the "best liars club" while we continue to seek a support system to keep our passion alive.

We part company for the time being, say so long, and make our tentative arrangements for our next golf outing. We reflect on the experience of the day while reconstructing both the good and bad moments. In our mind's eye, this now becomes the springboard for preparation for that next round of golf. It gives us an opportunity for rejuvenating our passionate anticipation for the next golfing experience.

I return now in my search for the answer to the fundamental question of what is *it* about this game that elevates my enthusiasm and desire? I know that my continued involvement, both playing and teaching, has become a powerful life force, to be experienced and shared with others. The involvement in my passionate pursuit of teaching and playing continues to open the door to the growth of knowledge. This newly found understanding brings me closer to my quest in discovering the elusive *it* factor of the game. The total understanding of *it* always is just outside my grasp. The more I give the game, the more magic is revealed challenging my desire and passion. Now I look beyond this day to what lies ahead as I plan my next encounter while searching the horizon in endless anticipation. My passion remains intact.

Learning to play in those magical flowing moments where oneness between the player and the game removes from us the human frailty in our wanting desire and allows for the freedom we seek.

Chapter Two

Spring Fever Forever

Awakened Spirit

Each new day is an opportunity for a new beginning just like the first tee of each round provides the chance for a new experience unlike any other. Each year, as I come out of hibernation from the long winter, I recollect the previous year's experiences while anticipating the new season's arrival. The time spent during the dormant moments of winter fuels my continued desire to stay passionate about my pursuit of the game. Many thoughts from the previous year manifest themselves in a rejuvenated love for the game. I have realized that staying motivated during this period of time off is very necessary. Slowing down the pursuit physically allows the mind the time required to internalize, evaluate, and realize an acceptance of new insight and direction. The cycle of renewal is then complete, clearing the way for the elation felt in my spring golf fever.

The necessity for continued contact with my students provides them with the inspiration that offers support for their own renewal. I can't help but think that we all need to discover a support system that allows us to recapture our inspired commitment. Staying connected to the intuitive sensibility of natural, congruent flow of body movement during the off season is the challenge at hand. The motivation that supports the passion must not interfere with the spiritual desire for continued pursuit. Therefore, if our passion diminishes our purposeful desire dissipates. How then do we stay focused without being overcome by a doubtful belief in our playability? This is the trick to keeping spring fever constantly alive. My desire is to share the understanding of natural ability that lies within the human spirit while helping my students move toward a method of play supporting passion and overcoming any self-doubt.

Self-doubt

Self-doubt often develops from a lack in understanding of how our physiology accepts natural movement. The human body is perfectly connected by the skeletal structure and the attachment of tendons and ligaments to the muscular system which allows for congruent movement. If the golf swing is not forced, but is generated by a full shoulder turn with a relatively steady head position, then the rest of the body will coordinate in a manner that will support a fluid connection. The club head returns to a square position ready to make solid contact with the ball. So, if it is that simple, why is it so hard to understand and even more difficult to remember? Internalizing knowledge leads to a routine which becomes second nature.

In order to accomplish a natural swing on a consistent basis, we must totally understand what I refer to as "the learning continuum." This has much to do with understanding how the mind works. We will cover this subject in more depth later in the book, but for now let us assume that we have the ability to repeat the same movement time and time again. If we assume this to be true why should we ever miss a single shot on the course? Furthermore, if we could achieve this mastery of repetition, would we risk boredom and lose the cherished passion? We must continue to find the ways and means to support our commitment.

A consistently renewed passion provides the capability to pursue our desires, effortlessly directed toward the level of accomplishment we seek. I have heard it said many times by my students and playing partners alike, "The harder I try the worse my game gets," or "When I just swing easy and try not to care so much *it* just happens." When I hear these statements I am brought back in touch with the true nature of the game. We need to set the doubt aside and just swing the club. Learning to play in those magical flowing moments where oneness between the player and the game removes from us the human frailty in our wanting desire and allows for the freedom we seek. Playing in the flow opens the eternal spirit to a total experience of exhilaration. However, not exhilaration that overexcites, but a human experience and a calm confidence in the process without focusing on results. We begin to close in on the heart of the game as we overcome our self-doubt. We must continue our efforts to get closer to this connected oneness that keeps our passion alive.

Moment's Time

Each spring the renewal of life is reflected all around us. This inspiring time would not be nearly as dramatic if it were not for the cold, dark moments of winter. The howling wind and blowing snow seems to penetrate the marrow of our bones compared to the serenity and hope of spring and summer.

During these dark days of winter, we should begin to train our minds to recapture the heights of pure pleasure and miraculous accomplishments from past rounds. Why not use this time in contemplative reflection recalling past experiences? Our belief is strengthened, the passion is increased in time for the return to the course in the spring. The human mind is very powerful and has the ability to control the outcome of our actions. At a later point in this book I will detail the process of guided imagery. At this point I want you to sit back and think of one of your favorite holes of golf. Close your eyes and be there. Bring up as much detail as you please and stay as long as you would like. Play the hole in your mind's eye and score the birdie. You can do this exercise daily and it greatly eases a doubting mind. Now you are ready to take it to an imaginary course. Walk its fairways, smell the fresh cut grass, feel the gentle, warm breeze, hear the sounds of nature, and taste the refreshing cup of cool water on a hot, humid day. These are experiences that are within your reach anywhere, anytime that can rejuvenate and keep the passion alive.

It is very possible to expand this process of mediation and guided imagery to mentally practice your golf game during the off season. Try taking yourself on an imaginary round of golf based on recollections of some of your best and worst moments. Visualize being on the course, hole by hole. This process will definitely build a purposeful experience while strengthening the anticipation of the upcoming golf season. Mental clarity leads to a heightened level of passionate purpose.

Golf requires self-directed psychological strength backed by an unfailing, positive attitude. It's our decision to take responsibility for our own destiny and accomplishments. The ability to maintain necessary endurance requires an internal support structure. Passion instills a strong value system based in honesty, sincerity, and open-mindedness. Our search for the truth will be manifested in results. Thoughts are formulated and developed through a process of growth and accomplishment. This holds our interest and supports the passion if we maintain a rational, objective, and efficient process that flows in an effortless manner. Through mediation our spirit penetrates and opens the vast possibilities of a peaceful pursuit. Now, we have an ability to move from an existence of hopelessly striving to effortlessly thriving while reaching a state of automatic, mindful mindlessness. Higher levels of accomplishment provide our passion with a renewed support system focused directly on the moment of contact.

Eternal H.O.P.E.

Our enthusiastic passion for life and living is reborn each year as spring emerges while hope is rekindled for the upcoming golf season. Golf itself is a catalyst for the hope and anticipation for future course events generating an enthusiastic spark. It is **hope** that has the power to support and renew our passion. If we think of the word hope as an acronym, we can break it down this way: "**H**" for **Health**—the very nature of the game requires a significant amount of walking. Studies have found that walking 18 holes of golf equates to 40–70% of the intensity of a maximum aerobic workout. Walking also has been proven to have a major impact on decreasing LDL (bad) cholesterol and increasing HDL (good) cholesterol while lowering triglycerides. If you walk thirty-six holes of a regulation golf course twice a week you could burn up to 3,000 calories. Eighteen holes are equal to approximately four and one half miles. This type of walking exercise increases your heart rate, gets the blood flowing through your vessels, and provides a marvelous cardiovascular exercise without becoming overexerted. You are not conscious of the exercise because playing golf is fun. Compare a four hour round of golf with the camaraderie of your playing partners to four hours on a stationary bike or treadmill and you will realize the advantage and appeal.

Being in the outdoor environment can also provide extraordinary psychological benefits. The beauty and serenity of nature can boost the spirit and lift your mood considerably. Spending time away from the troubles of life, completely immersed in the golfing experience, will reduce stress, a serious factor in both mental and physical health problems. Another aspect of a healthy body is the proper stretching and exercising of all the muscle groups. A golf swing, when properly carried out, provides a congruent, interrelated exercise of almost every muscle in the body, all at the same time. Golf integrates a beautiful combination of aerobic and anaerobic exercise while providing relaxation and social interaction. The company and emotional support of likeminded people aids in psychological well-being. The concentration required for the various aspects of the game calls on a mental acuity that helps to maintain or increase the clarity of our thinking. Additionally, golf can help us develop patience, compassion, perseverance, determination, and a host of other human values important to the support and quality of our human spirit.

My firsthand experience with heart disease and the medical intervention that followed provided a commitment to wellness that I now cherish. A new determination to maintain my own health has instilled a passionate desire for proper nutrition and physical conditioning. Golf has now become a motivational force for achieving optimal health and physical fitness. Through my own experience, I made a commitment to expanding my coaching and have become a certified, optimal health coach. This decision has allowed me to help others commit to lifelong well-being. Achieving good health has had a major impact on my purpose, self-esteem, and passion for everything I choose to pursue. Hope always fills the future with an optimistic outlook.

"**O**" is for **Optimism**. As we look around us in today's world, there are many reasons to be pessimistic. Maintaining an optimistic attitude is essential for our emotional well-being. Golf, like no other sport, requires an eternal optimism to carry us forward. If you think about it golf is the only sport requiring you to go and hit your mistakes. These errant shots often produce situations that require a positive attitude exceeding any level of reasonable sanity. However, it is this very aspect of the game that tantalizes our hope and stimulates our passion. Our occasional, miraculous, recovery shots, often outside our normal ability levels, renew and support the depth of our passion.

Striving for the lowest score possible is a rather unique aspect of the game. Most sports and almost all games, including the game of life, are about acquiring as much as possible. Having the least number of strokes is a very reasonable concept once we are introduced to the game. If we study it a little deeper though, we begin to realize our desire for the fewest strokes possible is exactly what causes us to try too hard. This, in turn, builds tension, decreasing our coordination, and often creating disaster. The optimistic attitude we have tried so hard to maintain becomes deeply disturbed. I always suggest that, for the good of the game, and the enhancement of our results, we should put out of our mind the artificially imposed standards, such as par, birdie, eagle, or the horror of a quadruple bogie. When we learn to support our desire with clarified intention, we have an opportunity to achieve the true satisfaction from the pursuit of the game. As this continues to occur, our optimism is supported and remains intact, ready for the challenge of the next required stroke. This often produces a spring like renewal of the optimistic nature of our spirit.

"**P**" is for **Play**. Participating in the game of golf refers to the activity as playing. This lighthearted attitude maintains a recreational mind-set toward the game. Many times, however, we are allowed to be controlled by the intent to achieve beyond our capability. Willful desire imposes on our playful nature. Perhaps we could achieve a more desirable outcome from an experience if our intention could be directed toward a more spirited acceptance of a playful nature. Removing any imposing artificial desire for perfection helps achieve spirited play. Instead, moving our thoughts to the required process provides effortless results. During the process of our strokes an inspiration for achievement is realized in our play. There is an ancient Indian text known as the Upanishads that declares:

"You are what your deepest desire is.
As is your desire, so is your intention.
As is your intention, so is your will.
As is your will, so is your deed.
As is your deed, so is your destiny."

A playful desire can surface in our golfing experience. The manifestation of a more relaxed acceptance and willful determination are capable of overcoming whatever we encounter. Intent to seek peace and harmony finds cooperation within the circumstances and situations that we confront. Results are no longer the purpose; the pursuit becomes the motivation. Our experience produces a more desirable outcome as the destination is achieved. Passion is reinforced through this process and even the worse disasters can be viewed as opportunities. These misfortunes are elevated to a higher realization of a natural, instinctive ability. In turn, hope remains constant and passion survives. Now, go out and play the game and bring the spirit of play into all aspects of your existence. The passion for your game will expand. You will influence those around you as your recreational golf experience helps to recreate the emotional, physical, psychological, spiritual, and ecological well-being, lying at the heart of all human needs.

Finally, "**E**" is for the **Energy** derived from our passionate connection with all that is golf. The life force moving all of us to action satisfies our desire, whatever it might be, and provides the fundamental energy. Power is created and directed by this force. If we take this power and organize it for a particular action, skill is developed. This allows for improvement through training and repetitive practice that develops into whatever level of capacity human nature allows. Capacity expands, generating more passion for our endeavor, energizing us to live life to the fullest.

Most of us possess the capability of increasing our output of energy at any given time. Why then do we limit our flow of energy? We live in a world that has become somewhat lazy and apathetic. If you listen to your peers, you've heard comments like, "I would like to do this or that, but I just can't muster the energy." You might have given in to those negative thoughts opting instead to just take it easy today. If you think about it, these thoughts are excuses blocking our choice of necessary action required to progress. We stagnate, becoming bored. How can we avoid self-destructive depletion of our desire while still achieving higher levels of ability and accomplishment? To answer this question I pose a question. How do we elevate our aspirations and reach our goal? Attitude affects our positive spirit, while the ego is supported through a pursuit of satisfying achievement. This energizes and manifests a realization of purpose that we attempt to accomplish. Now we enthusiastically allow ourselves to pursue.

As we begin to aspire and become completely involved in the total nature of golf as a holistic recreational activity it provides a remarkable support system for the human spirit. The further we immerse ourselves in the deeper purpose of play, the more we feel lifted from the routine of our day-to-day existence. The relationship with the game easily begins to spill over and affects all aspects of our lives. Whatever the pursuit, we examine the opportunities, while clarifying our accomplishments. We prepare for the task ahead, not losing sight of our aspiring goals. This builds and rewards the passion for the cherished times spent on the fairways and greens of our lives. Occasionally, we are challenged to recover from the depths of the rough while still providing an experience of elation stemming from the possibility of miracles.

The hope that exists within the infinite possibilities of the *it factor* provides opportunity and realization from a finite nature of an eternal human experience. Our passion is free to live on.

Transformation

As a child, when golf first came into my life, I would look forward to each spring, wishing I had been born to parents who lived in a warm climate year round. Living in the Northeast is not exactly conducive to winter play. As I matured, I discovered that the cycle of the seasons presents opportunities to connect with and respond to this process of transition. Each spring provided me with a sense of recommitment and redirection. Through the snow and blustery, cold weather, my anticipation and exhilaration magnified the intensity of desire, breathing enthusiastic new life and passion into the pursuit of my game.

Just as we witness nature coming back to life, we have an opportunity to open ourselves to a seasonal metamorphosis. Our own rebirth of excitement is supported for the upcoming summer. I always had an intense interest in the natural environment. I found the transformation of the many species of life forms existing on a golf course to be fascinating. As the caterpillar is born it is released from its egg. Genetically programmed it gorges itself in preparation for its reincarnation within the confines of its cocoon. We too are offered a release from the confines of our protective, winter habitats. The transformation into dedicated students of the game begins a seasonal journey of metamorphic progression, an evolution toward renewed individual beings. We too can wipe the slate clean and begin again.

As the new playing year surfaces our recommitted efforts and energies thirst for the acquisition of new knowledge. I often recommend that we establish our goals for the coming season following through with adequate practice and play, remembering to seek the assistance of qualified instructors, whenever needed. These efforts provide us with an energized reward as our spirit filled moments of exhilaration and profound satisfaction materialize. The continuation of participation through the season releases our predisposition for a metamorphic growth providing grander moments for future play. A self-actualized understanding of the process toward higher consciousness rewards the season's transformational growth. This increased capacity for physical, intellectual, and divine levels of our game is connected through a newly discovered capability.

Anticipating the new season's metamorphosis allows our transitional levels of acceptance to take place. As our current habits dissolve, replaced with higher levels of efficiency, we must yield gracefully to the changes we encounter; always willing to let go. There are times we feel we are going backward. At that point we must acquire the new awareness and capability that we desire. If we allow for a willing acceptance of the process, we will move forward.

When we permit the evolving new player to yield to the process, we then exercise imagination to run free, creating the vision of any future achievement of our purpose. Expectation of challenges and resistance should be expected, but outcome is welcomed. Overcoming the struggle is worth the effort. It strengthens us in preparation for the next cycle. As the process evolves awareness of the fundamental truths hold consistent in our game. Becoming a fully realized player transforms the experiences of the past season. Gradually we begin to re-evaluate the results and achieve our transformed capabilities. Now we prepare for the new cycle of evolution, through our unending capacity for growth and development. Once again, we move through the next cycle of time, distancing ourselves from the game, as the days grow shorter. Passion for the next season has time to reflect until our golf fever again intensifies with the anticipation of the next year's upcoming opportunities.

If we can allow the adversity to inspire, rather than destroy, then we will gain and grow in our human capacity. When we attach ourselves to an understanding that the disaster of a bad stroke produces a new challenge and the possibility of a miraculous recovery, then we are moving to a more comprehensive understanding of what it is.

Chapter Three

The Cornerstone of Passion

Content of Character

As we go through life, we are confronted with a variety of experiences presenting both opportunities and challenges. Our minds are constantly infiltrated by an ongoing barrage of thought impulses. Conflicting reactions are created by choosing the directions of pursuit in our personal growth and accomplishment. It is imperative to maintain clarity of thought, which supports a fundamental consistency that allows for decisive action. When we hold on to a guidance system structured with stable belief in an underlying value that we are attempting to achieve, the foundation that builds support for our pursuit is reinforced. I refer to this as the "cornerstone of passionate intent." With strong core values we are able to internalize a guiding force, which supports congruent decisions and actions. Our desire for accomplishment flows effortlessly and allows the emergence of intensified passion. Belief systems based on personal growth and achievement are anchored by strong, clear commitment coupled with the power of personal values.

The game of golf is supported by the highest level of honesty and integrity. A clearly defined human value system is imperative if the player is to become totally involved and committed to the full participation in and connection to what the *it factor* of our game requires. Our pride of participation in the total nature of the game demands a complete understanding of the etiquette and rules of golf. When we conduct ourselves within the bounds of behavior dictated by values we free ourselves to interact with one another, with the course environment, and with the respect that they are rightfully due. Our self-esteem provides strength of character and passionate connection to a purpose. If we take the time to build the cornerstone with personal values and affirmations supportive of the majesty of the game, our passion allows the spirit to soar.

Growing up, my fascination with the game left nothing to my imagination; my desire to learn always ruled. The word integrity was already a part of my vocabulary as early as age four. My earliest memories quickly recall those times in my life. I vividly remember conversations with my grandfather, as we sat cross-legged on the floor of his apartment, "watching" his beloved Brooklyn Dodgers playing ball on the radio. Yes, that's what I said, watching the radio. He would talk about the lack of integrity in a bad call and what he believed to be the inexcusable behavior of the players and the fans. Popie, my endearing name for him, in his own special way, was my first role model. As my interest in golf blossomed, I clearly identified with the code of conduct demonstrated by players and fans. Displayed clearly was the epitome of the word integrity. Golf provided a value system protecting me from bad choices in other aspects of my life. Thanks go to my grandfather. I would have loved to play a round of golf with him. Hopefully, you've had someone in your life like my Popie.

I continued to internalize the etiquette of the game, trying, whenever possible, to instill the importance in my students and playing partners. Etiquette is truly nothing more than common sense. Rather than spending time detailing all of the aspects of proper etiquette here, I would suggest that you take on that responsibility for yourself. Instead, let me examine the fundamental human value system acquired and supported by a well-formed relationship with what golf has to offer. When our beliefs are in alignment with our desire to achieve and grow, our value system becomes the structure supporting our path to the unfolding of the desired results. This, in turn, will lead to achievement and growth in our capabilities.

Tempered Desire

Our fundamental decisions and choices in golf and life, properly developed, provide an unwavering support system for which we are willing to strive. Accomplishment in golf can sometimes be achieved in an effortless manner. Our intended desire to make a certain shot or sink a long putt seems so natural that we wonder why, at other times, it becomes so difficult. There is a mystery existing in our intent to accomplish each desire brought forward in our consciousness. When desire for results becomes too controlling we experience a lack of the achievement of intentions.

At other times, when we allow ourselves to attain a relaxed, more meditative state of consciousness, a state of mindful mindlessness permits the achievement of miraculous results. In these rare moments, the mysterious veil concealing our desire is lifted for a moment, allowing a connection with the deeper secrets of the *it factor*. The key to obtaining our inner most desire lies in the ability to become one with our fundamental value system. This provides the necessary strength of conviction for achievement. Patience and acceptance of outcome allows for the achievement of results without the interference of desire. We want success so badly we are likely to try to over-control the process in an effortful manner, often resulting in disaster. This type of experience on the course will negatively transport our state-of-mind, easily destroying the pleasure of the moment. This sense of despair must be released as quickly as possible.

We must now regain focus, positioning the recovery shot into acceptable placement to score to the best of our ability. If we can allow the adversity to inspire, rather than destroy, then we will gain and grow in our human capacity. When we attach ourselves to an understanding that the disaster of a bad stroke produces a new challenge and the possibility of a miraculous recovery, then we are moving to a more comprehensive understanding of what *it* is. Many of life's lessons are often learned. As our strength of character is challenged and continues to grow, passion is lifted and achievements support the potential for infinite growth. At the end of the day, we are better for our experiences.

Being in the Game

There are times playing golf where we become totally immersed in a sense of well-being and satisfaction. It seems that nothing goes wrong and all is right with the world. We begin to wish that the round would never end. These are the times when we become one with the *it factor*. *It* does not have to be analyzed, contemplated, tampered with, or adjusted in any way. *It* flows as a stream flows, without thought or intention. *It* just happens. We are now in complete alignment with our core values. Our enthusiasm for life and participation in the moment produces an access to a divine guidance in our actions. Complete acceptance of the result leaves us with an acceptance that whatever happens at that moment, our shot is meant to be. We choose to effortlessly move on accepting our circumstances without frustration or anger.

I have witnessed some simply unacceptable actions by players on the course. There is no room for a display of out of control emotions. This behavior only reflects back on the player exhibiting it, providing no relief or cure for the disappointment with the result. The poor choice of behavior disturbs other players. We have a responsibility while playing with others to assure we conduct ourselves in a manner that supports enjoyment of the time shared. We must learn to maintain composure and overcome adversity with dignity. Our own composure reflects back on us and reinforces the structure of our being, cementing the integrity of the cornerstone. Success in life will come to those who demonstrate perseverance in the face of disappointment. Rather than crumbling, we must remain clear-headed, and tap the dynamic power we all possess. The ability to resurrect our belief, ignites the passion, and supports an enthusiasm that helps us endure any hardships of fatigue while keeping the desire for expansion and growth within our spirit. This is what constitutes the "re-creational" golfing experience. We now experience being in the game with the necessary passion bringing us ever closer to our search for what it is that connects us to *it*.

Handicapped by Our Handicap

The golfing experience incorporates a system of equalization of abilities, allowing all players to compete with each another. The player's handicap is adjusted in reference to par on any given golf course based on a difficulty rating for that particular course. Many times, we use this system to describe our playing ability. Players often reference their handicap when asked about how well they play. Low handicap players fall into a certain range typically between zero to ten. A mid-range player would be between eleven to twenty and a high handicap player is considered twenty-one and above.

This is a good and fair system, but has some fundamental flaws limiting the potential of the players' desire to expand their playability. The handicap can subtly impose a limiting belief and the player achieves only to the level represented by their handicap. The question is can we overcome the self-imposed psychological limitation on our potential? Is the continuation of progressive growth fulfilling the human desire to achieve to our fullest potential? When we think of ourselves within a certain class of players we easily become complacent. This leads to apathy and eventually disinterest. We only stay totally energized when we continue to strive for higher levels of capacity. The yearning for expansion within the context of the human experience adds exhilaration to our passionate pursuit of life and living. Remaining aware of the restrictions imposed, by limiting beliefs and responding with openness for setting goals and objectives will release us from the restraint of our current condition.

We must maintain an awareness of the limitations imposed on us by social structures existing in our life experience. This becomes true not only in golf, but also in life, as we interact with each other in a desire to achieve self-improvement. We continue to sort ourselves out into classes based on the perception of self-worth. So, we go on handicapping ourselves thereby imposing self-concept on what can be achieved. Human condition is open to a wealth of opportunities controlled only by the choices we make. It is very easy to say, "I can't do this" because of some belief we have in a limitation that we are convinced will hold us back. This becomes obvious in my experience as a golf instructor. The initial prevailing attitude of my students reveals an effort on their part to be positioned in such a way as to provide a protective mechanism, excusing them from their expected failure and lack of ability. I find them so eager to please me as their instructor, not wanting to disappoint, that they easily lose sight of our basic relationship of teacher and student. I always start out by helping them understand that they have no responsibility to me to achieve at any particular level. They are then freed to share in a cooperative partnership of experience while building the necessary understanding of body mechanics and swing structure that assures their success. By exposing them to an understanding of how their brain processes information and how learning takes place, we can move past any restrictions to the "continuum of experiential learning," which is the basis of all my teaching.

I believe we are all handicapped to one degree or another. Many of these handicaps are distinctly definable, while others are self-imposed. We should only be concerned with how to find a way past them. Later in the book I will be going over my methodology. At this point I would like to relate the experience that led me to an ability to cope with my handicap. This process emerged from a personal necessity and desire to self-educate and overcome the restrictions of mild dyslexia. My learning difficulties encountered in grade school required extra help classes, which isolated me from my classmates. The stigma of being sent to remedial help classes devastated my self-concept. At the time, dyslexia was not yet identified or understood and I was simply coded as a slow learner. I owe much to my fourth grade teacher, Miss Wallen. I am grateful for her sensitivity and understanding to this day. She was a beautiful, young, passionate teacher with endless enthusiasm for her students. Her demeanor of kindness and her ability to identify exactly what each of her students needed was remarkable. At such a tender age she became the love of my life. There was something she saw in me for which I thank God.

As I entered fourth grade, I was extremely introverted and lacked all understanding of my own self-worth. I wore glasses from the time I was in first grade, which at the time was not normal and definitely not fashionable. My deficiency in seeing put me in a state of conscious inferiority. Miss Wallen saw past all of that. She recognized in me an unusual, creative ability to overcome difficulties and discover my own coping mechanism. She asked me to stay after school for additional help. In short order these times became very special. We would have our little chats. She quickly realized that I had many interests beyond my fascination for golf. The outdoors was my friend and I had many collections from nature. I loved tropical fish, collected stamps and coins, and was quite proficient with my "Duncan yo yo." When we talked about my interests, she realized my exuberant passion for sharing my knowledge. Miss Wallen gave me my first opportunity to teach. My fellow classmates became interested in my hobbies. Through her commitment to my need for social acceptance, she decided to provide me with time each week to share my interests with the other students. I came out of my shell and blossomed that year. She allowed me to learn and achieve in my own way and in my own time. I only hope that all who read this book identify with a teacher as capable as Miss Wallen.

The point of this story is to introduce a concept I have developed and have the privilege of sharing with my golf students in a meaningful, long term, learning process. I owe much of the development of my methods and my understanding of the teaching and learning process to the seeds that were sown in fourth grade. I would like to dedicate my teaching process to that marvelous teacher who allowed me time each week to share my passions with my classmates. This formed the cornerstone on which my teaching rests today.

Interestingly enough, that year, our class was asked to participate in the actual laying of the cornerstone of our newly constructed school. To this day my thoughts are often rooted in the magical times of the 1956 school year. My hopes, and dreams lie embedded in the school's cornerstone to this day, which by the way, includes my treasured Duncan yo-yo.

What I discovered and developed is really quite simple, but clarifies a methodology that is easily followed. The motivational need when learning anything must elicit enough interest to energize our desire. Then we pursue our goals through a clear process, support a focused purpose, and maintain a passionate involvement. I have found in my ability to teach golf, a mission of providing a recreational outlet that penetrates the human condition and lifts the spirit. In learning the various aspects of the game, the student has the opportunity to raise self-esteem and tap into beliefs that carry over to all aspects of their lives. The "re-creation" of passion and desire leads to the realization of human potential. What I offer is a tool for continued long-term learning. I will elaborate further on the specifics of the method, but for now understand it this way. If you can conceive it, you begin to perceive it and then you start to achieve it, at which time you truly believe it. Now, you can totally receive it, but unfortunately at times deceive it. Occasionally you must go back and retrieve it. Each time you go through this continuum you will get closer to the mastery which never is totally conquered. You will now be a little closer to a comprehensive understanding of whatever *it* is. As this happens your passion expands in your continuing quest for fulfillment. Never again will you allow handicaps to handicap the ability to grow and progress in the game of life.

The Cornerstone

So what is our deepest desire that entices us to continue from one day to the next? What supports our hearts and minds in maintaining a balance of emotions as our pendulum swings from the exhilaration of perfect contact to the disastrous outcome of the missed three foot putt? There are those times when *it* all seems so absurd. Why are we expending so much time and effort? Occasionally *it* becomes so compelling that the game is all there is. Nothing else seems to make sense. We gain a resolve that isn't found as clearly elsewhere in our lives. A golf shot, to which the game owes its life, desire, and plan offers up a divine insight into the basis of human nature. We are energized and the structure of our character is grounded in the material content within the cornerstone's integrity. Play becomes a manifestation of the divine and not just for the sake of satisfaction of ego, personal gain, reward, or result. We become connected with the energy source that our game owes its life to. Passion continues to prosper and grow, allowing us to participate without questioning, moving gracefully from shot to shot, making strokes of calm tranquility at times both good or bad.

In aspiring for further achievements, we come to realize the possibilities of where the game will take us. This, in turn, releases new bursts of energy to strengthen our spirit and produce an exponential growth in new accomplishments. We play in the zone and do not falter. The spirit is now reaching a new level of expansion supported by the structural integrity of our cornerstone. Materials that make up our cornerstone are an aggregate. They contain the elements of intellectual thinking processes, physical strengths, combined with a coordination of balance. Psychological sense of well-being and spiritual connection to a higher source of inspiration must be maintained in proper proportion.

This provides the integrity of substance for our support system to be properly enclosed by the strength of the cornerstone. It remains up to each of us to design and maintain this structure for ourselves, calling on whatever resources exist in the way of instruction, equipment, facility, and social engagement. We must, however, in the end, be true to our own nature. The paths in life offer many choices. Paths are many, but truth is one.

The clearer the mind-set the more predictable the outcome will be. Our ability to organize our efforts opens the potential to connect with the divinity of the force. This is supportive of our infinite potential.

Chapter Four

Quest for the Secret

Source of Consistency

As a golf instructor, I have had the pleasure and the responsibility to introduce a large number of beginners to their first golfing experience. My interaction with them has provided me with a significant appreciation for and understanding of how their minds work. As I witness the evolutionary comprehension of their purpose, process, and pursuit of golf, I am continually invigorated with my own passion for the game. I have reached a point in life where my teaching provides as much pleasure as my playing. My own personal growth as a teacher and player is largely due to the trust my students place in me as their mentor and friend. This supports the further research necessary to expand my understanding of the students needs. As the connection develops, I transfer the mechanical, emotional, rational, and spiritual aspects of the game inspiring their passion for learning. Through this experience, I have grown in my understanding of how information is processed and capability is acquired.

There is part of the mind that allows for an automatic, intuitive response joined with the congruent, flowing movement of the body. This is observed in routine, daily activities. When the student gets out of the car and walks across the parking lot to the tee, they don't think about putting one foot in front of the other, it just happens. This is instinctive. They don't think about breathing, they just breathe. This is how it is in nature. The tree does not contemplate its growth, it just grows. The squirrels don't justify how many nuts they need to stow away for the winter, they just go on diligently getting the job done. The world of nature outside of the human being does not rationalize and take decisive action, it simply responds to its circumstances without contemplation. Learning to play golf requires a significant amount of this non-rational, reactionary response to function properly. The challenge is how can this response be taught and learned.

As intellectual beings, we seek out knowledge in a determined "need to know" fashion, easily overshadowing the instinctive sensibility necessary to comprehend the process of ball striking. When a student first comes to me, they want to be taught. They seek the immediate answer to all of their swing problems. It is my job, however, to allow them to discover a learning process. This is accomplished by providing students with the opportunity to treat the golf swing as an experience. They are allowed to understand the combination of total body motion, rhythm, and a natural, unhurried, coordinated effort.

What they need to understand is that the swing is much more natural than we are led to believe. Our normal thought process suggests that if the ball is going to go far, we have to swing hard. This is our number one misconception. Fundamental humanness positions us in a manner that allows our ego to truly believe its satisfaction is all that really matters. Due to our determined, forceful nature, we attempt to control every outcome. We try to make things happen. Golf, however, defies this logical thinking. When our mind, body, and spirit are in sync, the magic appears. The sense of flow and oneness with the perfect contact satisfies the soul, and for that wonderful moment, we have connected to the nature of *it*. Once again, we are recharged by the successful outcome of our effort. If we can learn to accept the experience into our being, capture it there, and establish recall within the senses, then we can grasp the secret.

Doing Non-doing

When we go out on the golf course on a beautiful, warm, sunny morning, we are filled with anticipation for an experience that will provide an ultimate enjoyment of the game. We begin to think about the possibilities that lie in front of us on this day. There are opportunities for grandeur and moments of disappointment. Frustrations are healed by the accomplishment of the next success. As we move toward the first tee, our anticipation turns to exhilaration. We tee the ball carefully, checking the proper height, locating the perfect spot on the tee box, and somehow feel the sense of rightness. We are eager for a decisive moment of contact.

Now we proceed through the pre-shot routine, rehearsing it again and again as if we were preparing for the lift off of the next space shuttle. After a few practice swings, we grow ever closer to a hopeful expectation. Carefully placing our feet in proper relationship to the ball, we take a deep breath, letting it out slowly in a last prayer for fulfillment. As we move the club slowly back from the ball, all seems right with the world. Our body mechanics seem perfect as we patiently transfer from backswing to downswing in an unhurried manner. This is truly a meditative realization of decisive action. The transfer of energy, originated from the coil of our body, is in concert with the coordination of the shoulders, arms, and hands. Effortlessly, we shift our weight in perfect balance producing powerful contact and acceleration through the ball. The satisfaction of the cracking sound at the moment of contact reverberates from within. The delivered perfection in achievement is now fully accepted as the ball flies long and straight down the fairway, providing our spirit the promise of desire and intent. It seems at this split second that there is really nothing to *it*. We've got *it* now—let's play!

When we are connected at this level of acceptance, we have reached a point of no longer needing to control the outcome. A flash of insight in understanding translates to our sense of trust and rightness within the ability to create a successful result. We become one with the force by exercising faith that the process lies within us and is supported by our intuitive sensibility. Our analytical mind must be put to rest. The very idea that whatever we want to do must transfer over to an attitude of "let *it* be done." When faith and trust are exercised to the fullest capacity we begin to align with an acceptance of our ability to succeed. Sensibility is activated and actions respond in an effortless, positive outcome. We just let *it* happen with no need for thoughtful control.

Wanting Desire

As we become more and more involved with the passion for golf, our wanting attitude can serve us well. However, we must be wary that the wanting is channeled properly, alleviating pressure of unrealistic expectations, while not creating anxiety and despair. Clarity of intention is made possible by a focus on the tangible nature of desired outcome. The idea of what we desire is not enough. It is only a passing thought. When the idea transfers over to intention, the process of achievement can be activated. A good example is our first tee experience from before. As we prepare for the execution of the stroke, we tend to hope for a good result. Almost, as I suggested, it becomes a playful moment of prayer. The golfer's prayer goes something like this—"Please, God, let the ball fly long and straight and should it not, let there be no one watching." Amen to that!

Once we move past the hope stage of mental preparation, we progress to a more productive state of being. When intention is motivated by aspiration, we transcend our desire for the result. The process of intention is freed from the pressure of the determined effort and unlocks a natural ability to experience the result that our passion seeks. What we aspire for tends to occur. We move closer to the spiritual essence of the desire, thereby releasing the life response for which we search. If we allow our aspiration to be clearly identified in the mind's eye, through a visualization process, then the possibility of a successful outcome moves to a level of probability. A rise in self-confidence comes with the clarity of expectation. This allows for the very freedom of execution that we seek. The awareness of this aspect of human nature is supportive of our self-esteem. Sincere sense of self-worth frees us from the bonds of ego; the constant need to justify our ability by seeking the outside approval from others is eliminated. Personal energy is now released in support of our passion. Wanting desire is channeled in a direction of natural, positive outcome without force or manipulation. Each stroke becomes smooth and clean. The soul is satisfied, the spirit is nurtured.

Holistic Connection

In the study of quantum physics experts have discovered the scientific support for the theory that we exist in the form of pure energy, both kinetic (in motion) and potential (at rest). So too does all of the substance that surrounds us. Energy provides a versatile dynamic and powerful part of who we are. We are provided with pure potential for whatever we wish to attract. This concentrated energy constitutes the very spirit within us. Our bodies, thoughts, and emotions are all outward emissions of the dynamic expended energy. How we direct this energy dictates the limitations of the positive outcomes that we achieve. The clarity of desire will ultimately influence the joyful quality of the life we chose to live. When the energy is obstructed by fear, anxiety, or worry, it becomes misdirected into defensive, manipulative, or protective postures. Our spirit is susceptible to discontent, illness, and lack of holistic connection with the life force. When we fully realize the power of the force within us, the experiences of golfing adventures continue to expand. An energy release becomes a conscious part of our everyday play, expanding exponentially. Properly focused, we witness the infinite potential hidden within finite existence.

When we are indecisive or protective, we are exposed to unresolved disturbances to our spirit, infringing upon the passion with self-doubt. Our mind needs to be trained to become non-judgmental in order to release the growing preparation and play. We must not be focused or concerned for the outcome. The energy field opens and expands the life force. When energy is released, proper intent and the timing of the results seem effortless in support of the purpose they serve. The resulting good fortune aligns with the change of consciousness within.

As we play golf, we travel through a range of emotions, which challenge any sane person's capacity to remain rational and stretch the capabilities of even the most gifted of psychologists. We must find methods that allow us to maintain composure in the midst of emotional shifts that impinge upon our spirit to the point of despair. The potential drain on spiritual energy brings us to our knees begging for mercy. We must find ways to maintain a true, rational mind, one that is in control of our emotions as we think logically, defining thought processes, and allowing for a flow of intuitive understanding. Golf requires an attitude of optimistic, rational thought that keeps emotional reaction at bay. We must acquire the ability to raise an inner strength of character and tap the highest qualities of the whole person. It is only through the difficulties challenging us where opportunity provides the change to overcome the adversities and connect with our higher self. When passion is strong the feeling of wholeness continues to support the integrity of our efforts. We move ever closer to the discovery of the secret which connects golf with the life force that sustains and guides us.

Oneness

Transcending the need for satisfying accomplishment in relationship to winning or losing becomes contrary to the fundamental nature of soulful, human experience. As we connect to our spiritual nature, we begin to identify with an eternal grace that focuses intention on a higher purpose of divinity. Developing the psychological strength of self-awareness creates harmony within the spiritual force. This provides the true sense of accomplishment we seek. Inner joy and fulfillment are effortlessly achieved as our days on the links become cherished moments of pure pleasure. The essence of recreational golf should strive to provide a journey away from the pressures of our everyday existence. The game's potential for restorative infusion of directed energy provides a soothing antiseptic for pent up anxiety and frustration. Immersed in the tranquil environment and connected with harmonious energy of our natural surroundings, we realize a very positive influence on our well-being. We are beginning to attach ourselves to yet another aspect of the *it factor*. By remaining in a state of acceptance, we are able to remove the self-blame and tolerate our human imperfection. We increasingly become one with the process without the necessity or concern for outcome. Our faith in execution remains whole without being in conflict with our emotional involvement. Complete clarification of intent in the pre-shot routine is imperative prior to execution. The clearer the mind-set the more predictable the outcome will be. Our ability to organize our efforts opens the potential to connect with the divinity of the force. This is supportive of our infinite potential.

As we connect with the divine aspects of ourselves, we discover the true nature of the God-given potential residing within each of us. The strength of our energy lies deeply within the universal connection to this higher source of creation. Regardless of our individual, spiritual, belief system, we should continue in amazement of the guidance that has led us to where we are. There are no accidents in life or golf. Have you ever asked yourself, "Why did I start playing golf in the first place?" Both intriguing and infectious, *it* draws us in with a magnetism that captures our imagination and penetrates our soul. If we periodically refresh the belief we have in ourselves, we recall some of the magical moments. These great shots help us come closer to understanding our own divine guidance system. If we take that connection one step further and deliberately nurture and refine its substance through our practice and play, we draw from this higher consciousness of our will. We identify more clearly with the wholeness of the experience in our golf and all of life itself.

Energy at rest remains at rest unless acted upon by an outside force. Conversely, energy in motion remains in motion unless acted upon by an outside force. As our will and desire becomes energized, we are guided in search of the secret of the game. Passion is supported within our full participation. We open to the spiritual force before engaging in the activity and we orient ourselves inwardly, instead of on the surface of life. By remaining silent within our mind, heart, and spirit, we will avoid impulsive actions bringing greater harmony to our decisions. As we seek to know all sides of the truth, the abundance of inspiration from the divine guidance comes into our lives with spiritual sincerity. We now understand how each and every situation we confront, whether positive or negative, serves a purpose in unfolding the wholeness of our being in golf and life. We can connect with our game and become one with an effortless, flowing motion of total engagement. The secret is revealed through our passionate pursuit as we connect to a process that supports the wholeness of our purpose.

Our authentic selves are connected one to another. Residing within the unique alignment is the oneness of the game that allows for learning from the inner core of our being to the outer limits of our heart's desire.

Chapter Five

From the Inside Out

Connection to the Source

When we play golf in search of its deeper meanings, we become entranced by a penetrating force and charged with a sense of mysticism, often defying logical acceptance. When we arrive at a point in our development where confidence supports consistency, we recognize the connection to an inner process that exists in the swing mechanics. Although the techniques have been meticulously taught and learned, until an automatic, intuitive response is acquired our capabilities are not expanded beyond a finite point. The journey does not provide us with an involvement that fulfills a passionate desire. We wonder what *it* is that satisfies the soul. At unexplained moments, when a resulting miracle is achieved, willful desire is satisfied by the power of faith and delivered by the divine guidance of perfect contact. At these moments, we are touching the essence of the game on a playing field of spiritual connection. Now, belief in our abilities produces the positive support, allowing the continued expansion of potential for achievement and growth. Moving past the simplicity of staying motivated to practice, we seek the discovery of inspiration revealed in the connection with the divine wisdom of a spiritual source within the game.

Motivation, to work diligently on process and technique, does not by itself achieve the depths of our full potential. It is only through the spiritual context of intuitive awareness that we gain the inspiration needed to overcome the task. As we experience a faith-guided connection with the spirit of our passionate efforts we come to understand the process. Energy is released within us that provides the unexpected, enlightened moments of brilliance. At these times, we are supported by the satisfaction of a soul that is in full alignment with the heart of the game. Connected to the source of inspiration, intended outcomes manifest themselves in an intuitive, natural ability. It is crucial for the golf student to satisfy their soulful desire to connect with the source of inspired play. In so doing, the golfer can transcend their selfish desire for results, which negatively affects their control systems and impairs their inner guidance toward effortless, realized results. Progressing past desire to control outcomes and the feeble nature of ego centered efforts to prove ourselves; we are released from the mortal need for material and physical achievement. Intuition is now activated. Inspiration opens the doors, building momentum, which releases our potential.

Comprehension that is achievable accounts for the depth of connection to the purpose of our play. By pushing the boundaries of effort, without concern for an evaluation of result, releases the potential for expansion of our capability. The final score is a mere record of result and has little to do with the inner exhilaration that comes out of the experience. As we learn to separate from the need to justify our stature by the number of strokes taken, we accept the rewards that come from a playful nature. Enlightenment is now provided by each moment of the golfing experience. The acceptance of spiritual connection becomes rooted ever deeper in the divinity that lies inside of us. We are released from the bondage of score and fully connected with a true purpose of play. Now we continue playing our game in complete support of our passion. The golf shots are traveling as they should, without any desire for artificial manipulation or misguided by last minute questioning. We become connected to a universal guiding truth, resonating through us, from the celestial rhythm within the music of the spheres.

Of Karma

Within the confines of cosmic awareness, we realize the infinite potential of the spirit's eternal nature. Discovering the unfolding of our insights opens the imagination to a mysterious connection to the divine potential. This is the key to the realization of one's destiny. As we move into an understanding of the flow within us, we are connected to the divinity of the golf spirit. This synthesis allows willful desire to be achieved. We are connected to our karma. Past experiences and present actions are aligned directly to future results. When put that way, our progress seems quite acceptable. If we learn from our mistakes and stay in the oneness of the moment, we reap the rewards in the future. However, it does not often follow that logical sequence. Something else is in control. If desire is not in alignment with purpose, achievement will be affected, creating a detour on our journey. We are out of the natural flow of karma. To understand our karma at the simplest level is to accept the truth in the phrase—you get what you give.

In scientific terms, we accept the concept that for every action there is an equal and opposite reaction, producing balance in our state of equilibrium. In the pursuit of our proficiency as golfers, we must stay conscious of the sense of balance. Physically, emotionally, psychologically, and spiritually, we must learn to prepare for the desired outcome. Results will not be produced to our satisfaction without the decision for an appropriate action, carried out in proper order. This activates karma in the process of execution. A passionate involvement supports the satisfaction of a perfectly struck golf shot. If, however, we are not properly prepared for the moment of contact, our indecisiveness throws us out of alignment with karma, resulting in a missed hit. The resulting shot can produce a chain reaction of karmic events taking on their own momentum. Our act of intention produces the impulse to engage in a process resulting in the outcome of our intended action. If we are clear about the connection of how the mind works in relationship to intended action, we maintain proper sequence through purposeful preparation. Mentally, physically, emotionally, psychologically, and spiritually, we then expect a higher degree of consistency in the oneness of the moment of contact. Try applying this realization to your process in golf and other aspects of life.

Preparation for Contact

Open to your thoughts, they will become your words.
Attend to your words, they will become your actions.

Refine your actions, they will become your habits.
Challenge your habits, they become your character.
Refine your character, it becomes your destiny.
Accept your destiny, it was created by you.
Anonymous

Mastering this realization will build your process of preparation for participation with patience, purpose, and perseverance.

If our intentions are clearly defined, we set into motion the "good karma" which provides our desired results without interference from outside stimulus. This, in turn, opens our purposeful play to the achievement of effortless involvement in a passionate progression. To the higher purpose of spiritual desires, we connect our passion to the divinity of the game. For each individual this search and discovery is slightly different. What is right for one is not right for all. I have discovered this clearly, adjusting my teaching process to the specific nature of each individual student. One of the aspects of my work, as a golf instructor, is allowing me to grow in my understanding of human nature. Within the uniqueness of each student lies their specific karma. My job requires assisting them in identifying their own authentic person, discovering their abilities, and fulfilling their potential. If I can accomplish those goals, their spirit will be lifted, their aspirations satisfied, and their passion inspired. Our authentic selves are connected one to another. Residing within the unique alignment is the oneness of the game that allows for learning from the inner core of our being to the outer limits of our heart's desire.

With Dharma

As we move through life, our actions, attitudes, physical presence, aspirations, decisions, and desires directly represent and reflect an image of how we are perceived and what we stand for within our personal character. How we carry ourselves in life creates our persona and identifies who we are as human beings. For the vast majority of us, there is no conscious development or deliberate effort to create this identity, it just happens. If, however, we make a decision to create the desired image we want identified, we accomplish a major effect on our ultimate destiny. We must be cautious though, we cannot be artificial in our efforts, nor project the image of inconsistency within any aspect of our true nature. Not attended to properly, we can come off as being artificial or phony.

The game of golf itself has a defining image. At one time, the game was associated with a certain social status that rejected participation of the common man. For women, it was almost taboo. It was rumored that the word golf was originally an acronym for "gentlemen only, ladies forbidden." This is a complete fallacy that I wish to dispel. My perception as a golf professional is that there has been a tremendous growth in the gradual acceptance of women in the game. Their dedicated commitment to golf has created new opportunities through their significant participation, adding to the popularity of the sport. In the early 1900's, men on the golf course were required to wear suit jackets and ties with knickers. This certainly must have placed restriction on a full shoulder turn and extension through the ball. There was also a time when the golf profession was not viewed as favorably as it is today. Club professionals were second class citizens serving the "gentlemen of the game." Today, while our dress code is somewhat more liberal than it once was, I believe in respect for the game, we should maintain an acceptable level of portrayal. When a student comes to me for lessons, I counsel them on their appearance so they may be well received on any golf course throughout the world. I have found that self-image supports commitment to individual passion and pursuit.

In Western culture, the more we live up to standards of excellence, the better we are able to relate to a professional attitude and demeanor. In Eastern cultures, this is taken very seriously. Dharma in the Eastern part of the world is looked upon as the only true path to fulfillment. In the golf world, the only way to fulfill our role of divine play is to behave within the context of our individual dharma. We ought to do the right thing, at the right time, in the right way, and for the right reason. Through this committed attitude, we maintain balance within our demeanor, not only in physical appearance, but also in total involvement with the sport.

Accepting a commitment to dharma in our conduct and intent is the critical component leading us to an authentic projection of our true self. If we are in complete agreement with the truth of our being, we are accepted as authentic and well conceived. Unauthentic beliefs of individuals are lost and consumed by anxiety, boredom, and despair. When this occurs, the momentum that otherwise would bring life to our existence is eliminated and even the deepest passion is destroyed. Now, we become vulnerable and seek relief to maintain an authentic life. We search only to relieve ourselves from responsibilities. Occasionally, we simply try to deaden the pain with various forms of self-abuse and attempt to remove conflict and drudgery of non-directed, mundane existence. Keeping enthusiasm in our life requires a conscious effort and an honest search for involvement in activities that ignite a passion. I was fortunately exposed to the intriguing nature of this game at an early age. As the years have gone by, the game has become my life force. Fortunately for me, golf, as a recreational activity, provides purpose and direction for all to share. It is a release for authentic lives well lived.

The dharma we are revealing becomes an expression of authentic, passionate involvement. The purpose is truthful, revealing a process which is easily accepted in the pursuit of each day's encounter. Our deep, inner beliefs and desires are manifested in the outer expression of who we are and what we stand for.

Inner Mind

Mental activity is an ongoing, never resting bombardment of thoughts that affects behavior. At times this becomes an uncontrollable influence affecting the momentary actions of our very existence. Oscillating impulses of elation or despair, worry, or fear dramatically affect the outcome of every living moment of our lives. We begin understanding how the inner mind works, eventually tapping into a way of deliberately influencing the desired outcomes. Engaging and exploring the deeper, magical moments that golf has to offer becomes a very useful pursuit.

As human beings we are motivated at the deepest level to avoid pain and seek pleasure. For the vast majority of us we do more to avoid pain than we do to seek pleasure. This is a concept that becomes very apparent on the golf course as we are confronted with the decisions necessitating an almost instant reaction to a given situation. A simple example of this occurs for most of us when confronted with carrying a water hazard to reach our target area. We know with absolute certainty that hitting a particular club a certain distance produces the desired result. We also know the exact distance precisely needed to traverse any obstacle. However, what happens in our mind's eye? We bring an image of the ball flying effortlessly across the water with a picture perfect landing, snuggling up to the hole for an easy tap in. It is easy enough to activate the power of positive thinking. We take practice swings in smooth, rhythmic pattern, positioning our feet in proper alignment. Now we can address the ball and start the club back away from the intended target. At this split second something happens. Our minds are instantaneously flooded with thoughts of the possibility of disaster.

We are now realizing the potential consequences of not making it across. The pain exerted on the weakness of the mind tells us to give it a little extra, just in case. At this moment, the kinesthetic response to the desire of avoiding pain of failed efforts kicks in, producing the exact result our mind was trying to avoid. The rhythmic ripples in the water tell the story. They radiate out from the point of splash down, creating a visual reverberation engrained on our minds of the painful experience of a double bogey and the loss of a new ball. Alas, we vow that next time we will lay up. What if, however, we could achieve the peace of mind that allows for trust and faith to carry us in the unfailing completion of willful desire? How can we transfer hopes and passionate dreams for success into potential for the greatness of the moment?

First and foremost, we must prepare ourselves through adequate instruction and practice. Beyond that, however, we delve into an understanding of the workings of the brain and how it transfers thought into deed. Developing a process allows us to become fully mindful, accepting our potential for achievement of any task without question, and allowing execution of the stroke to exist in a meditative state of "mindful mindlessness." We are less likely to change our minds by second-guessing when we achieve this condition of a "relaxation response" and are able to realize our heartfelt desire.

I have often heard my students say that they have "half a mind" to attempt this shot. They are confronted with the difficult decision of overriding the fear of failure with the exhilaration of success. It is the old adage heard at the beginning of each ABC Wide World of Sports, "The thrill of victory or the agony of defeat." The creative right hemisphere of the brain has all the confidence in the world in the capability and possibilities presented in the moment. The left, logical side says, "Yes, maybe, but I have the evidence of your past inadequacies that reveals a strong probability of failure." It is at these moments our spiritual faith is squelched and once again our full potential is challenged. We resort to a defensive posture and avoid the pain of our inadequate effort. Consider the existing possibilities if we fully exercise the potential power of the depth of our inner mind.

Outer Limits

All of human existence has been filled with accomplishments that are seemingly unrealistic and impossible at times. The doubter looks on from the sidelines with a critical contempt for the obscurity of a new idea or concept. Regardless of whatever ridicules the great achievers faced, they would forge on, undeterred in their efforts to achieve whatever they believed possible. Nowhere does this become more obvious than in the spirit of the amateur athlete attempting to achieve at a world-class level. The sheer determination of the figure skater dreaming of the possibility of landing a quadruple jump was once thought to be impossible. Not too long ago the triple jump was only landed by those considered at the top of their sport.

What we are witnessing now in various areas of extreme sports is challenging super human capabilities beyond the rational thoughts of the common man. We see this innovative thinking pushing the spirit of humanity to an ever-expanding potential, an infinite possibility of reaching inside of ourselves, touching our heart's desire, and supporting our belief in what is possible. There exists within each of us an untapped ability desperate to be released. If we are willing to connect with the necessary resources and open ourselves to our potential to achieve spirit filled joy, we express the achievement of our outer limits. I have an ever-expanding commitment to this incredible game and what it offers to each of us, regardless of ability. This belief that I carry within my teaching provides inspiration and encouragement to the students that I have had the privilege to teach.

Over the past fifty-seven years, my relationship to golf has gone through a transformation and a huge growth in comprehension. I realized the farther I reached for an understanding of the nature of *it*, the more *it* requires of me in my personal quest. The passions I have searched for in the ever so subtle and intriguing elements of play have helped me realize a newly found desire to dedicate my efforts to a new challenge. At the age of sixty-three, I am embarking on a new thirty year career goal to leave behind my own legacy of understanding and inspiration. In doing so, in my own humble way, I am on a personal venture to open the door to those who will follow. What I have laid out in the writing of this book is part of my promissory note, as well as a self-imposed responsibility, expanding my influence beyond my own personal finite existence. I only hope that it is accepted with the same sincerity as it is intended. I fully expect that I can achieve and maintain an energy filled mind, body, and spirit to radiate my own passion and inspire all who come in contact with me.

A distinct beauty of the game lays within its spiritual essence that provides players with a heightened enjoyment in participation. As a teacher, I have had the privilege of working with students of all ages and capabilities. Unlike many who share their knowledge, I find inspiration in each student's progress. Regardless of their previous experience, I remain dedicated to the challenge of opening their eyes to their possibilities for greatness. I have never had a student who didn't achieve an enthusiastic, child-like response to some level of miraculous achievement. I have witnessed achievement in an uplifting, spiritual awakening that reveals enlightened understanding as if a light bulb is turned on. The a-ha moment of accomplishment inspires imagination and motivates the willful desire within.

Outwardly, I hear my students say, "Now, I've got *it*." As their facial expression illuminates, their inner spirit is saturated in support of their growing passion. This is the opportunity existing for each of us who love the game to tap into a life response within our experience. Through the achievement of physical, mental, or spiritual accomplishments, we align ourselves with the outward reality of corresponding energies that are generated within the divinity of our makeup. The very first time we tap in a six inch putt and listen attentively for that marvelous, rattling sound, as the ball settles into the bottom of the cup, we open ourselves to the possibility of world-class achievement. Passion brought us to the game of golf and it is the game itself that gives us what we need to keep the passion alive. All we need to do is open ourselves up to the possibility of letting the nature of golf penetrate our spirit. The soulful requirement of the divinity within our true nature extends to the outer limits of the fully realized individual being. Continuing the search for how the game provides this type of involvement opens an opportunity for self-discovery. The "re-creational" support for the wholeness within our unique being allows for the passionate release of *its* deepest inspiration. Purpose becomes clear as we become inspired from the inside of our being to the outward expression of what we hold to be true and authentic.

Part Two

The Purpose

Playing the game of golf has many purposes. For some, golf provides a recreational outlet, for others it presents opportunities for camaraderie and socialization. There are those whose proficiency allows them to compete at high levels of amateur ranks or professional play. Still, others participate in casual events for business reasons or fundraising activities. Regardless of their reasons, their actions and demeanor on the course demonstrates their attitude and determines what they gain from their golfing experiences. There are some, however, striving to get something more out of the game. If we pay a little more attention to the subtleties within the nature of golf, we discover possibilities for deeper connections to a purposeful reflection of life.

Realizing this association offers opportunities for life-changing involvement, eliciting a journey into an understanding of our nature found at the core of our authentic selves. As we begin to discover a true purpose of play, we realize expanded abilities that affect our potential in a very powerful way. A deep yearning for meaning and purpose challenges our intellect, psyche, and spirit to relate with the cosmic connection of oneness with all existence. Searching for the truth lying beneath the surface of the game we begin to find a deeper understanding of what *it* is that has captured our imagination. We have the potential to be lifted to a higher plane of human capacity. The game builds our self-esteem gradually, overcoming any possible self-doubt. *It* clarifies our identity and provides a new level of self-respect. As we grow closer to the source of the inspiration we see a reflection of who we are in relationship to our game. Perceptions of our experience, played shot for shot, hole-by-hole, and round after round, provides us with the acceptance of our frailties. Our inconsistencies can be forgiven as our development unfolds. We examine this connectedness of our individuality within the universal order of things. A window opens to the true quality of our unique character. Realizing these opportunities, we are led to an expansion of our purpose. Learning the many life lessons that are offered, we have a chance to reach a true sense of spiritual fulfillment and emotional satisfaction. The challenge is ours to embrace.

Discover your own destiny as you define your directional path. Knowledge is pursued and purpose is clear as the passion for life's lessons from the game defines our authentic selves.

Chapter Six

The Search for Authenticity

Natural Play

Discovering our own personal authenticity in relationship to how we play golf becomes the key to understanding the spiritual essence of the game. The ability to create our desired vision broadens the perception thereby expanding the possibilities of achievement that we never thought possible. The forces existing within our play, both seen and felt, are revealed allowing us to work with them, rather than against them. A deeper appreciated awareness of the game's unfolding events are more easily aligned with and accepted. Becoming authentic in our play begins by searching the depths of our being and discovering who we are. What are the traits we personally hold to be true? How have learned behaviors and habits affected our attitude and formed a personal state of consciousness relating to the game? Understanding the controlling values, beliefs, and motives provides the guiding light. We establish and apply these signature strengths to an authentic goal. As our confidence grows, achieving a released freedom from the entrapment of the ego, we develop a calm humility. Then we are free to play from the core of our nature.

While developing authenticity, we respond more to the intrinsic motives that arise from a realization of our individuality. We begin rejecting the regimented *how to* of life and dig deeper into the *why to* of golf. Continuing our search for true identity, we see the genuine value lying within the quiet, yet vitalizing serenity. We achieve a lasting relationship with the fulfillment and self-confidence brought from the game and overcome our anxiety and self-doubt associated with missed hits. Our spirit is opened to a higher purpose of involvement as we focus on a desire to achieve authenticity in our play. Intent reaches toward an enlightened clarity of purpose that inspires our inner spiritual being. When we play from our authentic selves, fully participating, the achievements are based on a well founded self-concept. The harmony within this balanced state of oneness synthesizes mind, body, and spirit to support our personal theories of knowledge and release an energy flow. This allows acceptance of our well chosen, enduring goals and objectives. In our own time, we play who we are as an enlightened golfer in a natural way.

Affirmed Intent

Our subconscious mind is a very powerful untapped resource. When properly activated, the mind releases an intuitive sensibility for creative reasoning. Ability affirms the intent and programs successful outcomes bringing whatever we desire into our lives. The subconscious mind, when triggered into positive action, draws attention to our task. Conviction of purpose satisfies intense desire, carried out in an unforced, natural manner. Our bodily action is in a cooperative connection to our thoughts. Practicing golf becomes imperative, if we are to achieve beyond a mere recreational pastime, and move to a level that provides satisfaction for our inner character.

This process allows us to begin clarifying our true purpose of participation and play. We grasp a better understanding of our capabilities to achieve the desired result. Our authentic self becomes clearer in understanding, providing us with a motivational force of unstoppable, forward movement. However, we must remain cautious, preventing any unrealized, negative input from seeping into the process. Our subconscious mind accepts as truth whatever we are thinking and eventually believes what is programmed thereby affecting our on course guidance system. We get what we asked for. This process applies to all aspects of life. Fortunately, we have the power to transform habits, behaviors, mental attitudes, and reactions to reshape our game, both on and off the course.

For proper acceptance, we must put ourselves into a relaxed state of physical, emotional, and mental stability. Learning deep breathing exercises is one of the best ways of accomplishing this state. Take a moment to inhale air through your nose until you fill your lungs completely. Hold it for a few seconds and exhale slowly through your mouth, as you count backward—five, four, three, two, one. Completely let all of the air out from your lungs. Repeat this process a number of times. I recommend several one-minute breathing exercises per day. This procedure is marvelous for all aspects of your health and wellness, in particular anchoring any selected positive thoughts. This helps reduce the effect of stressful situations through the affirmation of your intent.

In your affirmations, create short sentences saying what you want realized. As an obvious example, when faced with any shot on the course, you should affirm your desire to permit the swing to happen with ease of flow and let the result be achieved. By allowing the swing to be made without overexertion, the shot will fly true toward your intended target. Continue to tell yourself, "*Let* it happen, do not try to *make* it happen." We must resort to a faithful execution that is based on a belief in the swing mechanics, ingrained by our past rehearsal and experience.

Within our conscious mind we are flooded with an ongoing barrage of self-talk. This inner dialogue, either positive or negative, depends on the situation at hand. If we allow the mind to run wild, it is like a mischievous puppy attracting trouble. Our thoughts are wandering on and off the course. We need to bring it back into focus on the task at hand. Any often repeated thoughts begin manifesting themselves within our experience, easily disrupting the integrity of the original affirmation. We see examples of this on every shot-making situation on the golf course. As we talk ourselves in and out of an expectation of the outcome, we continue to be inundated by an acceptance of the possibility of disaster. This must be overcome by continually taking control of how our subconscious mind is programmed. The conscious mind is clear about the intent accepting the integrity of our authentic self. The purpose remains intact, in spite of disruption within our momentary state of being. Only then we begin to gain control of an ability to manifest results through faith, trusting in our intuitive capabilities, thus tapping into the law of attraction.

Sincere Success

Each day as we go out into the world we are provided with opportunities, challenges, inspiration, heartache, and joy, generated from our experiences and the relationship we have to them. At times, we are so determined in our desire to achieve a certain goal or accomplishment that it continues to slip from our grasp. We become so success driven that we do not recognize what our situations finally provide in the achievement of true success. What do we sincerely want out of any endeavor? Golf is a mere microcosm of life itself. It is a useful tool, teaching us how to achieve and appreciate the true nature of a successful experience, regardless of the outcome.

How can we allow for a realization of success while not trying to control a game that is impossible to master? Is it the achievement at any given moment, or is it something more important than accomplishment alone? We have all heard the old cliché; it's not whether you win or lose, but how you play the game that counts. The reason we play is always subject to change. There was a time in my life when all I wanted was to become a tour player. I diligently and constantly practiced every aspect of the game. Mainly self-taught, I was immersed in my pursuit and consumed with acquiring knowledge. Due to financial restrictions, formal training was not a reality. I reached a level of playing capability both respected and admired. However, I never felt successful down deep in my soul. There was always something missing. Fortunately, as disillusionment for competitive achievement increased, it was replaced with a deep desire to help others embrace the challenges and dignity of the game that had become my life force. I arrived at an enlightened awareness to help others find the knowledge to expand their enjoyment. This provided far more joy of accomplishment than any number I could have posted on a scoreboard.

To inspire another and raise their level of awareness of their potential has become my true and honest passion in life. I had the good fortune of discovering this sincere connection with my authentic nature. Clarity of purpose supported my passion for making a difference in other peoples' lives, while providing them with inspiration to carry them forward. Through my deep connection with the game of golf, my inner spirit was released from the desire for solely personal achievement. I have acquired the true inner freedom of a successful endeavor.

Becoming detached from the compulsion to satisfy the egocentric need for recognition allows for a deeper purpose to emerge. The life fulfilling substance provides the support for true success found at the core of our spirit. We are now able to turn the playing of the game into a fundamental belief system, while forming our own judgment of success or failure. The decisions we make in the course of play are based on an individual understanding of what is right without fears or doubts. This state of mind provides an unlimited access to an inner awakening of who we are as participants. We form our own judgment of the success in each endeavor. How can we achieve this freedom of inner self-reliance? It takes a unity of ability and desire to expand concentration through mediation, visualization, and affirmation, which supports an inner peace and acceptance of our fully realized accomplishments. This, in turn, brings us ever closer to our true nature as players of the game, clarifying authentic purpose.

Limitless Consciousness

Our conscious mind is one of continuous, relentless activity. Thoughts, for most of us, enter our minds in a haphazard manner. Many of these thoughts become useful while others are just momentary flashes of possibilities. Remaining fully conscious from moment to moment requires a precision of attentive awareness and control over our focus on the requirement of the task. Golf, perhaps more than any other sport, requires a concentrated moment of connectedness to the integrated forces of mind, body, and spirit. The more we connect all of our senses with the realization of the moment and block out the impulses of irrelevant thought, the more we expect timely release of natural, compatible cooperation with our total capability. Most other sports are reactionary in response to another player's involvement. Instant subconscious reaction is required at precisely the right moment to counter the effort of the opposing player's purpose. Golf, unlike so many other sports, is predominately a solitary effort. In order to achieve our desired outcome, we must be totally committed to the intent, while releasing the tendency to over-control the situation. This requires the connection to the honesty of execution which authenticity supports.

The inner power we all possess lies in a relatively innate state usually not activated. To truly achieve the growth in our ability and realize the purpose, we need to be clear about what these inner powers are and how to tap into their energy. One of the most obvious of these powers is concentration. We develop the ability to close off the bombardment of non-authentic thoughts, as we open the freedom within our consciousness remaining attentive to our purpose. Through the use of guided imagery, meditation, and relaxation response training, we open the pathways to the inner true power and energy required for progress. To begin our efforts connecting with the inner powers, we clarify a willful desire to support purposeful pursuit. If we consciously activate inner strength to make clear decisions and take decisive action to handle any situation regardless of the difficulty, we are able to tap into our determination and resolve. This requires an authentic activation of self-discipline, foregoing any tendency for instant gratification in favor of a higher purpose.

To fully release the passion lying within one's purpose, our imagination opens to handle many of the challenging moments encountered. Training of imagination through exercises related to a relaxation response leads us to surprising answers to even the most difficult of situations. Our imagination is not restricted to visual images. We learn to use all of the senses to conjure up sound, taste, scents, physical sensations, feelings, and emotions that dramatically affect any desired outcome.

We support persistence and motivation, reignite ambition, and develop self-confidence with an authentic realization of limitless consciousness. When we are able to connect to these inner powers, we then should expect the peace of mind necessary to detach from any of our human frailties and fears of failure. This restores the inner balance so necessary to fully realize and support a conscious acceptance of our unlimited potential.

Lessons Played

From the days of my youth the lessons I have learned and the game I have played have provided a consistent support to my life. Sitting here in contemplation of the next season, I wonder if it could possibly be any better than the last. My mind flashes back through so many fine memories of the past year's pleasures. I have grown personally from this game and learned continually about human nature. Yes, this game has become my teacher of life, my guru that motivates and entices my spiritual connection to search deeper for the purpose of life's true meaning.

I only hope my students and those who share in these thoughts, that I am putting out to the silent breezes of cosmic energy, realize their life's purpose and are inspired to *go fore it*. So, as I continue my search, I ask myself at this time of reflection where was I, where am I now, where am I going, and where will I be? There was a time in my life when I was so motivated by the thought of escaping into retirement, allowing me to play unlimited golf with my lovely, wife Beth, that I would gladly have just dropped out. However, the realization has appeared, particularly in the past seven years of tenure at Winding Hills, which has made me aware of the strength in the connection that I have with my life's purpose. In the next thirty years, I am dedicated to a newly realized life's mission. Retirement will only come when the work is done. The way of the committed nature of my game has become crystal clear.

I think back now and recapture some of the thoughts and reflections of my days on the course, the practice tee, trying to recollect what I have learned and what was taught. Why has this seemingly unimportant recreational pastime made such an impact on my life and motivated my desire to such a high level of dedication? How do I allow a natural unfolding of life while trying not to over-control or manipulate my true destiny? In what ways can I pursue a natural growth with a sense of rhythmic flow required to achieve a sense of spiritual well-being and enlightenment? These and many other questions have come to mind setting the path on the road less traveled to a destination just beyond the eighteen hole. I open myself now to a clarification of consciousness with a clear path off the tee, down the fairway, onto the green and into the hole. Discover your own destiny as you define your directional path. Knowledge is pursued and purpose is clear as the passion for life's lessons from the game defines our authentic selves.

*Activation at its highest level of intent challenges us by the most intense
awareness of need. This is the do or die moment of truth. During this time,
significant adrenaline flows, producing super human capabilities. All doubt is
cast aside as we fully accept the responsibility of the moment*

Chapter Seven

Conscious Awareness

Non-duality

Intriguing mental abilities emerge while engaging in the process of learning, practicing, and playing golf that require concentration and focused awareness. Clearing our minds of outside interference and distraction joins the oneness in the moment of contact with all of our human sensibility. Achieving this level of congruent interconnectedness of mind, body, and spirit touches a sense of non-duality that allows for total engagement. Released from a controlling desire, an experience of effortless motion allows for our spirit filled involvement. Through these magical moments, we achieve an ultimate experience of freedom and understanding with a deeply meaningful purpose of passionate involvement in our game play.

Accepting the game of golf at this level of awareness allows an escape from the over controlling ego driven individuality. We become fully aligned in the totality of pure awareness that activates and stimulates our senses. Sensibility is allowed to grow through a totally involved process. Eliciting an ongoing supportive advancement of ability and capacity provides a complete acceptance of our full potential.

The roots of philosophy of non-duality came from the Far East which suggests everything that exists is an integral part of one spirit. This concept has been accepted for centuries in that part of the world, however in Western cultures, more attention has been paid in recent years. Beginning to understand this sense of oneness connects our power of concentration, attached to the process rather than the result. Detachment from the useless efforts produced by the belief that a control of outcome is achievable provides freedom from a dominating intellect. Intuition activates an inner awareness of spiritual certainty. Relief from the dominating conscious desire to manipulate intent is accomplished. We realize the capacity to gain control by losing control, fully experiencing the joy of accomplishment that connects our spirit to play. The golf experience has now touched the awakening and enlightenment that moves toward the deeper meaning of purposeful play.

We all possess the capability to quiet our mind and slip into the space between intellectual thoughts, allowing for the realization of full potentiality. The mind is directed to a peaceful, silenced state of acceptance and achieves a natural flow of coordinated effort, if we prevent ourselves from trying to manipulate the outcome with deliberate actions. Excluding a dominating thought process allows for the successful accomplishment of each stroke. Now, moving ever closer to a state of non-duality allows the inner spirit to become one with the game. As we are finally able to rise above our intrusive, negative thought patterns, the initiative to quiet an imposing mind-set returns us to a center of oneness. The game is now played with a fully internalized awareness of confidence demonstrated by our capability to produce results.

We challenge ourselves to search deeply inside for the source of thoughts that dictate each action as we discover the acceptance lying at the core of our capability. Finding a natural flow in our golfing life we move closer to understanding the non-duality of purpose for a desired result. Ultimately, we achieve the sought-after purity which opens an awareness of our intent.

Mindful Mindlessness

As we play golf, our minds continually are challenged to stay focused on the task at hand. Yet, at the same time, we are constantly stimulated by remaining open to the unlimited potential of the creative impulses, helping us to progress from shot to shot. The creative mind is more spirit driven and continues to be open to moving outside our individual comfort zone. This allows for the full realization of ultimate potential. It would be a mistake not to open ourselves to risk for the possible reward of an exhilarating and inspiring playful attitude. If we continue cautiously attempting to achieve a successful outcome, our growth as players is stifled and we easily slip into a level of ambiguous apathy in our play. This eventually may lead to a deterioration of spiritual passion, and puts us at risk of thoughtless involvement. However, what exists within the mindless aspect of our being is strength of subconscious reality. When properly nourished, this becomes very useful in freeing our inherent natural abilities.

In my own play, I accept and understand there is a definite, intuitive sensibility in overcoming my fears and anxiety that shift my willful desire into a defensive state. Understanding a resourceful power of the mind and engaging in a trusting attitude with a worry-free acceptance of the outcome creates results more remarkable than ever expected. Surprise can often happen. What a lift this provides for the psyche, as a new vision of possibilities is gained. This mind-set is second only to the power of the spirit becoming mutually supportive as a master of the thought process. Mindful efforts must be properly channeled to immediate, conscious thoughts, and allowed to pass through to the subconscious mind without negatively influencing any actions.

Focusing within the conscious mind, we detail the complete attention to power, while not concerning ourselves with the outcome. Allowing the mindless subconscious to accept the projected imaginary is real and probable. Efforts are carried out without restriction. The necessity of ambitious, sincere effort to rehearse mental transfer from mindful desire and intent, to subconscious acceptance of probability, dictates the capacity of our gamesmanship. If our belief in the actions and situations manifest themselves through strength of commitment, then the shift to mindless control produces the natural flow of developing habitual nature fully activating our capabilities.

Occasionally, students try convincing me that they have no imagination, however I tend to disagree. I do find however, that it is seriously suppressed in many people. My teaching has convinced me that this ability must often be actively developed. The various exercises I utilize in my educational process dramatically improve the ability to concentrate. Many students gain a certain conviction in their expectations providing them with the determination to shape and improve other aspects of their lives.

As my students become more successful in their achievement, I witness a joy in participation that continues to expand. The feelings accompanying their past success are nurtured, becoming the magical force of their future achievements. If I, as an instructor and coach, move them to an intentional, conscious effort that evokes their intensity, they are able to achieve to their ultimate potential. A possibility exists to saturate the subconscious mind with a new desire for capturing the exhilaration of success in their conscious mind. This assists the acceptance, without resistance, while releasing their awareness to the flow of their intuition. Their ultimate purpose of participation in the game is strengthened through the pure enjoyment they have experienced in the mindful mindlessness of their growth.

Clarity Conditioning

Maintaining a clear, uncluttered, calm demeanor, while being totally focused on our immediate need for achieving a task requires the highest determination of purpose. This realization opens our potential with an ease of execution and produces the consistency we are seeking in pursuit of the game. Our purpose must remain clear. We must be totally honest with ourselves about what we are hoping to take from each golfing experience while remaining open to giving back through the determination to learn and grow. Inevitably, we can't take more than we give in life. This creates an imbalance in the cosmic laws of the universe. The Golf Gods could get you for that—bad karma! When purpose is in alignment with needs, we expect continuing rewards while enjoying unlimited potential for satisfying experiences. The game we engage in is totally ours, free from outside influence. We take full responsibility for our actions and decisions without the negative effect of inner anxiety, fear, frustration, or blame. In spite of changes within any circumstances, we maintain continuity within our purposeful pursuit. The internal certainty and conviction lying within allows us to maintain total ownership of our game. The clarity of playing golf with purpose allows for an impenetrable depth of realization, as we experience kinesthetic flow to full capacity.

We begin to achieve anything we wish if we establish a clear directional choice. Our commitment to assessing a situation as we make a clear decision allows us to accept full responsibility for the result providing freedom of play. If we continue playing golf with an arbitrary acceptance of results, our game play meanders with aimless inconsistency and encourages an internalization of self-doubt. Not being deliberate in your decision is in itself a decision. A defining clarity in identifying exactly what results we expect provides a release of an intuitive capability and allows a swing or stroke to occur without the interference of an over-controlling mind.

Your golfing experience requires immediate decisions and clear thinking as you stay in the moment. You begin to witness a measurable growth in your achievement committing to a precise focus on what you want to accomplish. This practice programs your natural swing to become directional without your conscious mind interfering. As you continue rehearsing this procedure, it becomes progressively easier and more accurate. You are ruling out all other possibilities, automatically attaching an assurance of the expected outcome.

A complete commitment to the nurturing of a clarity of vision and desire must remain open to all possibilities. This allows for the creative input that is imperative before a course of action is too quickly accepted. You may remember some past experience in which you faced a challenging trouble shot requiring a solution that often stretches your imagination. At a certain moment, your decision became obvious. You made the swing and you were rewarded with a miraculous experience. It was not accidental. The circumstances required a clear, precise decision captivating your complete attention. The situation demanded a clearly focused thought process that conditioned appropriate *response ability*.

If we tap into past experience, draw from it, and apply it to all shot making situations we can adopt a clear decision making process that is ultimately responsible for a progressive advancement in our game. We are now becoming true players, achieving a conscious awareness, and bringing a purposeful realization to the enjoyment of our golfing experience. Our capacity of purpose is conditioned by an ongoing commitment to practice and play.

Feeling the Flow Zone

Existing within the higher self-awareness is a very unique type of intelligence, transcending thought processes, which enables the body, mind, and spirit to unite. This state of being brings on instant clarity and focus, neither requiring nor eliciting any effort on our part. We capture an instant, yet spontaneous sense of exactly what to do and how to do it without any concentrated effort. Activation at its highest level of intent challenges us by the most intense awareness of need. This is the do or die moment of truth. During this time, significant adrenaline flows, producing super human capabilities. All doubt is cast aside as we fully accept the responsibility of the moment. The results are exceptional achievement and feelings of unparalleled ecstasy as the forces outside of our own awareness are mutually cognizant and aligned.

Still, at other times, this quality of alignment emerges from a place within us of pure relaxation and acceptance. A completely natural involvement requires no extra effort or thought and allows us to go about our business. The job needs to be done without thought, contemplation, or preparation, we simply get it done. The outcome from this state of oneness produces an equal level of exhilaration that affects our fulfillment more by simple acceptance of the do-ability and serenity within the moment. As we achieve our result in this situation, we tap into the timelessness of the event and capture the intrinsic motivation of being completely and effortlessly involved in the accomplishment. Our minds have become crystal clear.

The state of flow zone exists for all who play the game between apathy of a task too easy and the anxiety of a challenge too hard. Achieving this state of flow is absolutely necessary if we are going to continue our search for awareness of our purposeful play. Achieving and nurturing a consistent state of flow must not be contrived. If we are going to capture it, we must turn our attention back to a conscious awareness. Our effort to elicit that state of the flow zone becomes crucial to the development of our golfing experience. The goal here is to keep emotion under control and avoid the high highs of super charged elation and low-key acceptance of happenstance while creating awareness that produces consistency of flow.

There are certain characteristics we need to be aware of to capture the flow zone consistently. As we begin to examine the characteristics required, we accept the absolute need to find a place of relaxation within us. We move with great ease in this place producing strength of commitment. As we seek to develop control of this peaceful state, we raise our level of confidence and acceptance of the probable result. Now, we allow ourselves to drift into the space between thoughts, absorbed in the moment of execution. Totally focused with precision and effortless concentration the need is satisfied without any outside interference. The entire process becomes effortless. We elicit a sense of finesse and grace from the awareness, outside of our normal thought pattern, regardless of the difficulty of the task. All anxiety is cast away. Our action becomes totally automatic as the game of golf becomes more enjoyable. Yes, we are in control of our play from the depth of our soul, however not from the imposition of willful desire. We then are in charge of our destiny. The authenticity of the process is totally within our grasp. We are free to attach to a purity of purpose with the playful nature of a child with a new toy.

Going Fore It

If we go back for a moment in reference to the *it factor* in golf, we begin to understand our relationship to the challenges golf presents. The ability to develop a positive attitude inspires a passionate desire to continue growth and achievement in the game. The array of situations and circumstances challenges our courage, but at the same time motivates our capability for achievement.

Regardless of the amount of experience or expertise, anyone who plays golf, whether on a course or at a driving range, is confronted with choices and decisions on how to play their shots. Depending on levels of confidence, belief, conscious desire, and willingness, their purposeful commitment is dictated by the passion they bring to the task. This, in turn, supports their actions and encourages the psychological satisfaction lying at the heart of their determined purpose.

Further examining the player's decisions, I have witnessed a vast difference in motivation for levels of achievement, ultimately determining the potential for advancing their ability. Over the many years of teaching the game, I have gained a great awareness of the various levels of need, desire, will power, and commitment controlling the motivational purpose for achievement. I have always attempted to accomplish a *go fore it* attitude. No matter what level the player is on, it is my belief that they should be raised up in their committed desire to achieve at the next level. Then, their spiritual essence connects their passion to their purpose, thus supporting the pursuit of their process. Achievement becomes the result *of* and not the purpose *for* their participation. This results in the natural growth of their involvement and the self-satisfying effect on their conditional well-being. They are continually able to let *it* happen without intimidation or fear of failure as they commit to the full follow through in their intent.

I realize through my teaching that there are various motivational methods that inspire my students. Their differing ability levels and personal attitudes require precise attention to their specific needs. For many, the self-imposed, limiting, defense mechanisms provide a reason for self-doubt. Many students have responded that they cannot do what I am asking. When confronted with the task, they try and simply allow themselves to do it. When they succeed, their protective support system is dismantled, and their enthusiasm exudes. I ask them, "Was it worth the effort?" They usually respond with a joyful chuckle and say, "Well of course, that's because you were here with me!" Interestingly enough, that very statement provides them with a defense posture and excuses their future anticipated failure. It is important to realize that this quirk of human behavior provides a pre-conditioned lack of belief in their ability to achieve. This relieves them from the responsibility for the expectation of success. I say, "Just *go fore it*," grow in understanding of what golf and life offer. No fear and no holding back. Play the game, whatever the game may be, and play it as if you mean it.

Going forward, it is important to understand, that at the depth of our motivation lays the fundamental forces of pain and pleasure. If we are not aware of it, we continue to do more to avoid pain, than seek pleasure, as was previously discussed. This aspect of our condition translates into the limiting defensive attitude that never allows us to reach the heights of full awareness of our capability. The protective shield must be lifted; risk must be taken to release the bondage of psychological self-preservation. If we don't try, we can't fail. Just go out and playfully *go fore it!* It is only then you will own your game. Decide to play golf in a state of conscious awareness with passionate involvement and a purity of purpose.

71

As we envision, wishing to achieve, and taking positive, decisive action we organize our efforts into a desire for accomplishment. Then, we systematically carry out our intentions with a preserving effort. We open ourselves to the potential design of the proper course and focus on a tangible vision of a resulting expectation.

Chapter Eight

Capability and Potential

Course Design

Continuing the search for clarity of purpose we discover a need to carefully assess our current level of capability and realize the potential for future achievement and growth. If we open our imagination to envision a course of play where the greatest ambitions and aspirations are fully realized, inspiration is energized providing the acceptance of possible accomplishment. The game of golf now presents the next level of acceptable challenge. Spiritual fulfillment comes with the expansion of playing capacity increasing and supporting a continued passionate involvement. Passion and purpose are now united and set on a course that is clearly designed. This establishes the necessary procedure to pave the way for an effortless pursuit of our ultimate hopes and dreams. Expansion of the vision of the possibilities strengthens our willful desire to overcome the challenges. A well defined course of action has now been thoughtfully laid before us. We are finally positioned to play away.

Taking the time to clarify and realistically examine our current ability level provides a motivational force that carries us forward. We make decisions to accept the challenge of rejecting any limit to a potential for growth. We push outside of the gravitational force of our comfort zone expecting nothing but the best results from our efforts.

Thoughts become clear enough to accept a newly realized possibility of playing capability. Seeing ourselves in this new way, we open the spiritual connection that allows for a successful outcome. However, this is not easy. It still requires courage and tenacity, as well as the unfailing faith that our desire can be fulfilled. During the weakest moments of hopelessness, which undoubtedly will come, our determination is challenged to the limit. Each time we ask ourselves to dig deep, and take action to regenerate the momentum; we are lifted up over the next disappointing experience. All of this serves us well, but as we continue our achievements, we must be careful that selfish ego does not begin to distort the purpose and turn the dream into a nightmare. Individual integrity has to remain intact and true to our purposeful play. Then, hope and faith carries us to new levels of joy and satisfaction supporting the spiritual fulfillment of passionate involvement.

Many of my playing partners over the years, when confronted with challenges, have often responded in a reactionary fashion. This, for the most part, is a self-defeating and unconscious behavior. If they were to respond with clarity of focus that allowed for a deliberate action their aspirations might be carried out without overreacting. Now the dreamscape of possibilities can achieve a more powerful support. As we envision, wishing to achieve, and taking positive, decisive action we organize our efforts into a desire for accomplishment. Then, we systematically carry out our intentions with a persevering effort. We open ourselves to the potential design of the proper course and focus on a tangible vision of a resulting expectation.

Dreams inspire us to believe that we have the potential to expand our abilities, and gain new levels of exhilaration. We chose to take decisive actions from our dreams in the hope of unlocking fundamental life forces which have a very positive effect on the evolution of our game play. Most of the outcomes in life begin with a decision to no longer tolerate our present condition or circumstance. As we look forward, we decide not to accept our current standard of play. Instead we take on the challenge of pursuing a new level of achievement. We begin expecting to arrive on the course of our dreams, realizing the capacity and potential lying at the fundamental root of our purpose.

Willful Focus

Growing in the understanding of the golf experience, we begin accepting the necessity to reach inside ourselves for a determination accomplished only through a deliberate and sustained effort to achieve the intended result. This determination strengthens the commitment to pursue goals and objectives while satisfying a wanting desire. This willpower moves us to action in all aspects of our lives. Of all the motivational forces, activation of our will is the most important support for determination and tenacity. Without a strong will, it is difficult to maintain the stamina required to accomplish the desires and ambitions while still advancing our abilities. During the most questioning moments, human willpower carries us on to overcome indecisiveness.

This power of the will is accessible and is equally important in all aspects of our lives. Without willpower, we tend to procrastinate over both minor and major accomplishments. High energy levels are required for us to remain focused on our active desires. Willpower is the mental force assisting us in most of our decisive actions, propelling us to act and to be motivated to follow through. The necessity for strength of will is critically important in our golfing lives, as it provides us with a courage and strength of commitment, to confront the challenges and disappointments that are consistently presented by our game.

As a golf teacher, my passion is renewed each time I work with a student who has yet to realize the depth of their inner will. The uncertainty that lies within the student is set aside, as an emerging self-belief strengthens their motivation. This begins to release the power of the will. In witnessing this inspiration and success, I further understand the strength that participation in sports in general, but golf in particular, has on the unfolding of their life force. Through my continued interactions with students, I realize how much I truly love the game. The transfer of knowledge provides me continued inspiration and strengthens my own passion. From my privileged vantage point, I observe my students' willingness to challenge self-limitations or physical handicaps. I watch as they accept the possibility of achieving higher levels of success while pursuing the game's pleasures. As the initial discovery and activation of their will meets with the challenge of the task, the presence of their disbelief yields in a rather natural evolution.

The student now experiences remarkable results through the decisiveness of execution.

Making a commitment to change a habit or achieve a new goal requires us to be in the correct mind-set. This is the first step in activating the power of the will. At first, it is a gradual process that feeds on itself and grows exponentially. Momentum is built supporting positive results. The growth process itself turns into an absorbing, exhilarating challenge, enhancing all aspects of life. This development of willpower lends itself quite nicely to the discipline necessary for sustaining our advancement of all aspects of the self-realization. It moves us away from a self-conscious belief and empowers the spirit with a desire to be actively achieving and growing. I believe in the power within the game of golf, if pursued with the proper understanding, attitude, knowledge, and commitment. It presents us with a recreational outlet that allows a personal and passionate involvement. This, in turn, supports every aspect of life. Willpower serves us well, seeking an understanding of our capability and potential. The purity of purpose continues to be manifested in effortless momentum, both in our golf game and all of life's encounters.

Intentional Being

Once we believe we can increase capability, our desire for expansion becomes important enough to move us in a direction of realizing our potential. We need to fully engage in the active, willful determination to structure the intention and pursue purposeful goals. When vision becomes progressively clearer, goals and objectives become precise. Our intention is focused on the specifics of the various aspects of the game, allowing for the accomplishment we seek. It is this precise intent, when properly maintained, that provides for the small improvement of techniques and mental acuity making the difference in the final outcome. We remain in touch with our emotional desire to achieve the result, but at the same time, we do not let it disturb the underlying intent. Much of the ability to grow in our pursuit of achievement lies within the mental strength of commitment to maintaining a consistency of positive thought. This provides us with a surge of energy which cooperates with our desire and attracts the exact results we seek.

Understanding the human consciousness is so important in golf because there are a tremendous variety of shot-making situations to handle. Quality of the life response is most highly fulfilled when we deliberately remain fully engaged through our intent. As our commitment to gaining knowledge expands, we put in the effort of consistent practice, allowing intention to become progressively easier to fulfill. At times, it seems that, regardless of the depth of our aspiration, we might not reach the result of the intended efforts. After examining our motives, we find that ambition has clouded over the true intention. To this end, we must exercise caution.

During a practice round, we have the opportunity to hit multiple shots from the same position, honing our focus on a precise desire. Then, connected to our intention, we remain focused from shot to shot. By consistently practicing in this manner, we are able to associate our intended outcome with the kinesthetic behavior. Utilizing this method of practice prepares us to elicit our intentions from an intuitive part of our being. These intentions become consistently positive and supportive of the belief in our abilities and potential. Our faith in the achievability of even the most challenging shot grows strong with confidence.

If we seek out our spiritually inspired nature and apply it to a receptive, divine, and decisive process, then trust in our natural ability is well served. We all wish for high levels of accomplishment equal to our intent. However, if this wishing sparks too much ambition, we slip dangerously into the responsive tendency of playing for the purpose of ego fulfillment rather than the authentic satisfaction of our pure pleasure.

Intentionally deciding to embrace the totality of what the game offers, we accept the responsibility of our disappointments, as well as the height of our grandest achievements. If we can gracefully accept and internalize the constants in the game, the best of intent is brought out. The purpose is supported and nurtured with very little conscious effort on our part. We are released from the restraint of any external demands and instead are more motivated, playing our game as a representative of who we are. The purity of our purposeful play perhaps holds up as an inspiration for others. The game of golf, thanks to its long tradition of integrity, rightfully deserves the respected stature it holds. Maintaining high standards of integrity allows us to have a pure purpose. Only then, can we play the game completely immersed in its wonders and joys, regardless of the final score.

Clearing the Way

Capability and potential are understood separately in each individual, in conjunction with needs, desires, motivation, passion, and purpose. As a teacher of the game, I attempt to elicit various responses from my students in hopes of developing their insight into what they want to receive from the game. What I generally discover is they possess a relatively low expectation. Students usually do not believe they can achieve great feats on the golf course and set very low expectations to avoid the pain of failure. Upon contact with the ball, they instantly open up to the possibility of higher achievement and enhance their sense of purpose. This expansion of awareness activates their imagination and awakens each individual golf spirit. As this process of realization continues the flow of energy begins to take over and enthusiasm is ignited.

What I have noticed in my many years of playing and teaching is the vast majority of people reach a certain level of play and stagnation sets in. As I mentioned earlier, I believe very strongly in the need to overcome these self-limiting beliefs, in order to release the creative spirit to all of the wonders in golf and life. My own passion and mission is assisting others in their realization and growth. I see people who have simply accepted a survival role, either consciously wanting to protect what they have already achieved, or unconsciously moving day-to-day, swallowed in an existence of apathy. They stagnate, focusing only on what's directly in front of them. My sincere wish for all who read these words is to look out to the horizon and think up. We are in a time when the only choice is seizing the moment and looking to the opportunities of the future. Golf will always be part of my internal support system and it could be in yours also. I always rely on the game of golf for its metaphoric relationship to life. The parallels are startling.

We make a clear, committed decision in rising above our current levels of achievement, expanding our quantitative and qualitative experience. Gaining the momentum for growth is critical to the satisfaction for which the inner spirit yearns. This provides the upward movement from our current level of ability. Caution must be exercised that this expansion is not just more of the same. There is a fine, but distinct, line between "perfect practice" and "practicing perfectly" in the notion of the five p's encompassing the personal, purposeful, passionate practice of play. Maintaining clarity within our desire is not simply supporting or defining the egocentric demands. We are able to tap the spiritual guidance necessary for achievement of a truthful realization. Achieving this new level of understanding, lives become restored by our faithful commitment to the realization of potential, while remaining true to the spiritual balance we seek. We move on in our evolution, to a higher plane of awareness of the circumstances presented in golf and life. A sense of underlying certainty of outcome supports a peaceful demeanor of acceptance. Purpose remains clear and unburdened when an ambitious desire achieves a higher level of capacity in an unnatural, artificial process. Our growth remains strong and vibrant, clearing a path along the chosen way.

Emergence of Energy

We are better able to reach awareness of an infinite potential and rise above our current playing level when we accept and connect to the golf spirit. This process flows as our energy source continues providing whatever support is needed for higher levels of achievement. This spirit contains a source of energy that overcomes any obstacle between the desire to achieve and the results accomplished. In making a conscious commitment to refueling this energy, we gain momentum toward our goals. We are assured of decisive actions required to support all of our endeavors through a purposeful pursuit. The self-determination to accomplish the task generates the physical energy needed to achieve the desired outcome. We get on a roll, so to speak and must keep our lives in motion to avoid a pattern that could lead to apathy, boredom, anxiety, despair, and eventually depression. The degeneration of mind, body, and spirit could follow. This cycle feeds on itself, leading to hopelessness, and a breakdown in our positive attitude toward life.

In a startling way, we witness this on the golf course, not even aware that it is invading our consciousness. The simplicity of a missed three foot putt leads to an emotional landslide, seriously affecting our internal energy source. This disastrous, downward spiral is set in motion and unless stopped, erodes our self-confidence. At these moments we must stop, think, and decide to accept our fate or look within ourselves to recommit our purpose and overcome the adversity. Once again, we establish an upsurge found within the spiritually, motivated belief in ourselves. We commit to the depth of our capacity that allows us to reconnect with our flow zone.

So how can we deliberately, at will, recharge the energy source lying dormant within our being? One of the most important ways to stop a backward slide of momentum is to stay in the moment and maintain belief in a holistic oneness of our larger purpose. This is nurtured by focusing clearly on the requirements of the task, while aspiring to carry out the necessary process with total commitment. A prevailing attitude re-establishes the belief in our capability and potential. Now, we are able to shift into a forward thinking mental position, producing a hopeful outlook that supports our faith. A new surge of energy is released. All too often, we believe our energy is finite when, in actuality, a simple, positive result activates the energy flow at any moment. We need to remain open to the opportunities presented. Full, intense effort, holding nothing back, supplies the necessary fuel for your next explosive growth expansion.

Many times when working with a student I become aware of their diminished enthusiasm affecting their committed energy level to practice and play. An altered state becomes necessary to overcome the fatigue of the moment and rejuvenate the necessary desire to continue their pursuit. This is accomplished by providing temporary relief restoring the necessary inspiration to move forward. What I recommend is that they sit down, close their eyes, take a few slow deep breaths, and go on a quick, relaxing, mental vacation. This method supplies their mind, body, and spirit an opportunity to escape the frustrating momentary thoughts. They can be somewhere in their mind's eye, away from the current conditions. Sights can be seen, aromas sensed, even food can be tasted as you listen to a special song. Once these inner feelings have been touched and relaxed they can return to the current moment with revitalized existence. Fully rejuvenated they are ready to enjoy the re-commitment and re-establish their cherished poise with the realization of resurging energy. This process raises their subconscious flow of desire lying at the heart of a larger purpose. Connection to the golfing life once again becomes the source of inspiration to their capability and potential to proceed.

The core of what we desire in life must be cared for in a deliberate manner. Awareness of our vulnerability to drift into states of weakened spirit must be ever present. If we continue to discover the ways in which we maintain enthusiastic involvement our energy emerges whenever called upon. As we witness the true potential purpose in life we are supported by the continued effort that our expectations require as we pursuit our game.

True courage is the ability to perform beyond expectation in the acceptance of fear. The head-on confrontation and ability to overcome adversity coupled with a composed attitude of determination is the true realization of any courageous act. Only through exposure to experiences that demand our fullest attention can we enhance our courageous playing ability and strengthen our confidence.

Chapter Nine

Courage and Confidence

Anticipatory Regret

Think for a moment of what life would be like if we knew that whatever we decided to attempt would not result in failure. Successful outcome would be assured. What types of endeavors or decisions would we be willing to take on and what kind of adventures would we experience if we had that certainty? If we were to take on the challenge and expand our effort with absolute belief in the advancement of our playing ability, what decisions and commitments would we make? In our golfing lives we are prone to avoid the possible disappointment, choosing instead, to accept our current level of accomplishment. We cannot be disappointed in our efforts if we do not attempt the task. Allowing ourselves to anticipate the possibility of failure, we also avoid the regret resulting from our decision and settle for our existing capability as acceptable.

When I was teaching in public school and my students turned in a project they often asked if "it was good enough" to meet my requirements. I responded by questioning whether or not it was good enough to meet their requirements. Most of the time they decided to continue working a little further on the assigned task. When finally completed, their satisfaction level was greatly enhanced. They moved out of their comfort zone and felt the true sense of accomplishment so necessary in overcoming the anticipation of a regretful decision.

Their courage and confidence grew as their passion for learning was stimulated by their personal satisfaction. They chose to take up the challenge and expand their capabilities.

We must understand that it is not a lack of ability holding us back from achieving our goals, but rather the fear of failure. Only by facing fear and following through on the intent can we achieve full potential. Rather than facing that difficult shot with anticipation of how regretful we would feel if we failed, why not attempt it with expectation of achieving our intended result? Embracing life at the highest level is one of the keys to a successful existence.

Think for a moment about the internal debate of what you have to lose versus what you have to gain. Replace the anticipation of failure with the possibility of success. If we continue to merely accept the status quo, we are settling for a life of mediocrity and survival, rather than an existence of expanded, adventuresome growth. Our efforts spent on improving the knowledge and techniques, while initially feeling burdensome, eventually are lifted, providing the effortless ability to grow and thrive as our lives evolve along with the game.

My suggestion here is that we apply this premise of expansion of the life force to all that we do. The effort put in pays back great dividends to our psychological well-being. We discover a life of vitality both in golf and a day-to-day existence. Energy sources are fueled with high octane providing the necessary internal combustion for the realization of our potential. Now, let us set aside the notion that if we make a decision to act, it could perhaps be the wrong decision. If we choose not to decide we do not have to hold ourselves responsible for a bad choice. This "anticipatory regret" is a strong force lying dormant in our subconscious mind. It can surface at any moment, to sabotage our future achievements. If we do not take the time to understand its power, we continue to recognize good enough as acceptable. This weakens our self-confidence and courage to act. As our search for purpose continues, we come to scrutinize our game in hopes of giving the best of ourselves in golf and life. In searching and challenging our current status, we reap the ultimate rewards.

Optimal Thought

Golf is one of the most totally fulfilling human experiences if we allow ourselves the freedom to accept and pursue it as a worthy endeavor. We realize that golf has the ability to lift our spirits to higher planes of consciousness when we open our minds to its value as more than just a recreational pastime. This offers us a clarity of purpose as we pursue golf as a guiding life force. When we first experience the game, there is a stark simplicity of thinking. After understanding the fundamental necessities of making contact, we begin to achieve reasonable capability to maneuver the ball around the course in one form of survival mode or another. As we have periodic moments of mastery, usually by accident, our mind is stimulated to begin a discovery process. This has a profound effect on the continued evolution of our desire to participate. Accepting the game in its totality opens the mind to possibilities that begin to appear. As we continue allowing the game to capture our attention, we change our thinking process and open up to the optimal thought patterns required to engage in a total golfing experience.

As the critical thinking develops, it affects every situation. We encounter a pervasive influx of mental activity, which continues to challenge our judgment. This causes us to accept, reject, or suspend our commitment of play and deeply affects the confidence in the perceived expectation of outcome. Self-doubt now feeds on the flittering thoughts from lack of focused attention. This ambiguity in our negative thinking affects conscious effort to act on the decisions required by the situation confronted. Our stroke is compromised by the infiltration of last second questioning. Within the pre-shot moments of decision, all relevant information is instantly internalized through all of our senses. Logic must be applied along with a broad intellectual acceptance and analysis of the situation. Critical thoughts and decisions remain focused, facilitating the almost instantaneous action required by the evidence presented. Each and every shot comes down to this specific internalization of the desired outcome through a process orientation. This then allows for the release of the intuitive realization of feel, often necessary to accomplish the task.

When confronted with the most challenging situations, we must be able to release our thinking from fear and anxiety, detaching from the negative expected outcome. The kinesthetic response alleviates the potential for disaster. We need to remain calm, allowing for the full acceptance of our capability. Experience is progressively conditioned to the process of decisive actions through the structure of our thoughts. We find the process becomes effortless and reassures us of the ability to achieve and expand. This, of course, increases the ever growing desire to play the game and opens us to a more enjoyable and relaxed experience.

The calculated decision to take our game to the next level through a critically developed thought process eventually provides an optimal relationship with the expected result. We embrace and connect with the mental aspects of the game. Remembering a worthwhile endeavor in life is always supported by the value we find in *its* purpose. As our critical thinking becomes clear, courage and confidence are optimized. Willful desire aligns with the clarity of our intent.

Serenity of Mind

When we are playing on the golf course, we could easily fall victim to a desire for achievement of ambitious goals. The inner mind understands and accepts that hope for a successful outcome lies just a little too far outside of our perceived ability level. We could become paralyzed by fear. Thoughts shift from positive encouragement to negative anxiety, leading us to possible failure. So how do we continue to stretch, moving outside of our comfort zone, while still expanding the potential experience? Do we continue to perceive that we are playing over our heads? There is definitely a disturbance in the force of courage, breaking the necessary confidence, while robbing us from the mental acceptance of our flow zone of play. We must strive for an inner peace and strength of mind to dismiss doubt and any vision of disaster.

The mind is powerful and provides us with the ability to achieve success that exceeds our perceived ability level. When we truly detach from our egocentric need to succeed and commit to the requirements of our situation, it becomes possible to accomplish a level of focus that moves us to a more accepting state of confidence.

During many of my playing lessons, I put my students in some precarious situations, challenging their courage. I have them hit multiple shots from the same position. With the pressure of perfection avoided, the stress is removed and the student has the potential for a positive experience. This relieves the fear of failure and allows for clarity of focus. I highly recommend this type of practice because it expedites the way we build self-belief and elicits an ability to achieve outside our comfort zone.

The courage to reach for growth requires the acceptance of fear. I have heard players say that they are fearless. This is as disempowering a state of being as fear itself. A player easily develops a haphazard attitude toward their play, by simply using an attitude of fearlessness in their efforts. It becomes their built-in excuse for failure. True courage is the ability to perform beyond expectation in the acceptance of fear. The head-on confrontation and ability to overcome adversity coupled with a composed attitude of determination is the true realization of any courageous act. Only through exposure to experiences that demand our fullest attention can we enhance our courageous playing ability and strengthen our confidence.

Our minds are trained to maintain a confident mental composure, pushing and challenging the abilities during practice sessions. As we begin to achieve repetition of success, we build and expand our reality of expectation. This affects our belief through the consistency of our results. These easily recalled accomplishments translate into peaceful acceptance of successful outcome. If we re-establish the experiences through daily practice, our mental images become stronger and more consistent. The clarity of expectation affects our attitude, behavior, and actions. The mind, body, and spirit connection achieves strength, and allows for effortless thriving in our pursuit. We now attract into our lives, as golfers and human beings, the desired corresponding events, situations, and opportunities. Courage and confidence provide the mindful serenity of our purposeful play. Faith in the outcome becomes steadfast belief.

Returning to the Source

When we seek accomplishments in life, with the sole intention of superficial recognition, our motivation is at risk, and our sense of reward wears thin. As we seek a deeper satisfaction, we are more spiritually connected to our achievements. Within our connection lies a sense of truthful pursuit coming from a divine, purposeful commitment. Our purpose manifests itself, resulting in achievements, realized with grace and humility. Rewards need no recognition from outside of us since the purposeful satisfaction is far greater than any outside commendation.

As we progress in our understanding of the *it factor* of golf, we comprehend the physical nature of the game. The efforts hold our spirit high with brilliant moments of achievement, and are occasionally dashed by horrific results, sometimes produced by an overconfident mind-set. At the root of our disappointment we find our ego's need for artificial support in its search for reward. It tells us that we hold the answers within ourselves, accomplishing anything we desire through our own determined efforts. Therefore, we deserve the outward recognition and respect for the results of our efforts. When we shed this delusion of grandeur we bestow upon our spirit the ability to make a significant move to higher ground.

Although we often hold a light-hearted attitude toward the concept of divine intervention that our cosmic connection can provide, deep inside of our spiritual essence lays a guiding force. If we allow ourselves the time and energy to reach within and exercise a process producing the mindful mindlessness necessary, we can connect to the flow zone of our spirit. In achieving this, we begin to believe in our connection to the eternal nature of our source. We are provided with all the tools necessary to play our game with grace and dignity, with calm demeanor, and ease of accomplishment. The Golf Gods will show us good favor and the rewards appear from the deeper aspects of our resourceful spirit.

We have the profound ability to alter any situation by simply changing the corresponding reactions. This type of control of our circumstances comes from the trust in the source of creation of which we are all a part. By re-establishing the understanding of non-duality, a trusting nature is supported. This provides the peaceful confidence necessary to attain courage even in our most desperate moments.

The game and our lives continue to unfold as they were meant to. When we connect to the source of creation in our pursuit of excellence, we open ourselves to all possibilities. Our tendency in our game is to try to control and manage the outcome. I suggest that we pursue the simple understanding that we must lose our controlling willful wanting to gain control. As we move ever closer to realignment with the source, we accomplish the effortless achievements that we seek. Courage and confidence are gracefully restored and accepted in the rightful way in which they interrelate.

Poised for Play

Understanding and accepting that the nature of our being is connected to a higher self, we transcend the demands of immediate gratification. Pure potential is opened without an internal, forceful desire to accomplish immediate results. Becoming more patient, we achieve a stillness and silence within our thoughts. The openness of our focused mind allows more acute awareness of the unfolding circumstances as we play our game. It becomes easier to stay in the momentary need of the required stroke. By allowing our inner poise to be nurtured, the decisions on our actions are affected by the highest order. Confidence in the results of our actions lies safely within the bounds of our positive, expected outcome.

The necessary tools to achieve a higher skill level through discipline and practice provide clarity of purpose. Power is developed that opens the secret within the spirit of our play. This leads us to an upward expansion of capacity, achievement, and support. Confidence grows as we exhibit higher planes of courage in our playing decisions. As character becomes an integrated aspect of the playing posture, we begin to feel the release of the creative, intuitive instincts. It is within the development of what becomes our game that we discover the truths in the evaluations and accept the growth in our capabilities. We become more empowered through a search and discovery of our playing potential. Now we seize the opportunity to face adversity and overcome the challenges while acknowledging with graceful dignity the disappointment in any negative outcome. On the positive side of exceptional achievements, we must keep those moments of magic under the control of a grateful acceptance of our good fortune and not be swayed by ego fulfilling admiration or reward.

When we are able to accept our achievements with the poise acquired on the higher levels of consciousness, we discover a reduction in stressful thoughts. The ability to silence our mind from the imposition of negative thoughts brings forth the courage to tap into the creative impulses of calm, collective, effortless play provided by the power of the golf spirit. The mind becomes ready to receive the accomplishments, achievements, and successes as a joyful, living experience. This becomes our ultimate, personal reward. There are times however, when our ambitious goals or desires are so strong and our visions of achieving them so clear, that there suddenly appears a negative fear that they may actually be realized. The intellect creates a subconscious dismissal of the possibility of accomplishment as a protective mechanism rejects our potential. Doubts and fears that arise are in direct conflict with acceptance of a positive outcome. We must remain open to growth, by analyzing the desire while accepting the responsibility of our newly found potential for personal expansion. If we remain poised and ready for the moments of inspired development, we are able to block the negative, intrusive thoughts, restricting our efforts of acquiring the potential evolution of our playing ability. We overcome inertia within our stuck state of being and graciously accept a newly found level of accomplishment. This capacity to accept the possibility is at the core of courageous action. When our confident spirit is supported, we continue to sustain the purpose lying behind the meaningful endeavors in life.

The chosen course is designed, constructed, maintained, and played with a well conceived intent. Using freedom of imagination continues your journey as you discover the destination and set a course of your own unique design.

Chapter Ten

Your Course Design

Setting the Course

As we position ourselves for the journey in life, with golf nearby as a trusted friend, we begin moving forward in joyful pursuit. Passion for play provides the necessary determination and energy to overcome any obstacles. We have become students of the game, always yearning to move forward with the foresight of an explorer sailing west to find New Worlds. Here lies a culture of the enlightened, spiritual connection to our love affair with the undiscovered truths, lying within the spirit of golf. As we set our sights and position the compass needle we cautiously search for a directional course for our chosen destination. We progress within the confines of a patient, purposeful flow. The game of a lifetime cannot be force fed with quick fix concepts or technical innovations. These too often claim to cure our ills. Even before being fully diagnosed, they manifest themselves in an unidentifiable misalignment.

Developmental time is of the essence to become the completely realized player you aspire to be. Remember to become an authentic participant. Your integrity must be supported by an unwavering value system that aligns with your purpose and passionate desire. Within this framework of full commitment, you discover a straight line of sight from tee to green. You become one with the game and with your way of life. If you take time to properly design your course of play, the peaceful evolution of your advancement remains clear of the hazards that destroy your scoring potential. If you continue to exercise patience a par round may exist in your future.

As you hold a stable position and focus on clearly defined goals and objectives you maintain your true intentions. The choices that confront you are many. Continue to seek your destination and stay focused on the guidepost of your North Star. Your willful desire and ambitious motivations carefully nurtured are properly channeled. They remain in alignment with the divine guidance of the universal force that runs through your spirit. When purpose remains true, and vision is clear, heartfelt desires become fully realized. The purpose is fulfilled and passion is ignited providing the energy source that supports our endeavors. We are all connected to this endless energy source.

The finite achievements that you have in life are all part of a larger expansion of energy that provides the propulsion needed for your journey. Opening to the spirit of your will, assures the positive results that become the manifestations of aspirations and desires. Effortless evolution becomes the outcome with no possibility of exhaustion or ultimate disappointment. However, difficulties may be encountered. These are placed to challenge tenacity and determination to discover all there is to learn. Face each difficulty in the positive light in which the Golf Gods intended and move forward, undisturbed in the ultimate decision to design your own course of action. Dignity will always be supported through an ever stronger passionate pursuit. The purpose in playing becomes clearer, as continued efforts are confronted with opportunities, challenges, disappointments, and exhilaration of achievement. The deepest, most meaningful desire may not be revealed by the exact course that was planned, but ultimately the discoveries that have been made are detoured in the right direction. The chosen course is designed, constructed, maintained, and played with a well conceived intent. Using freedom of imagination continues your journey as you discover the destination and set a course of your own unique design.

Your Personal Best

Regardless of where we are at any given point in our abilities, there is always room for improvement. As we design our course of action, we must regard infinite expansion as an absolute requirement. It is so easy to say to yourself "that's the best that I can do" or "I have tried my best and failed." But what happens if we simply changed those statements by adding the words "at this time?" With that addition, we change our momentary state of being to a possibility for future expectation, compelling us to achieve. Our personal best should always be just outside of our grasp. The goal should be to take small steps toward improvement, while building a consistency in the learning process. The stability of our game is then structured on a foundation of steady expansion of our capability, recognized by the small trophies along the way that never tarnish.

To achieve your personal best, you must evaluate your strengths and weaknesses. You must have a clear view of a starting point. Professional evaluation of mechanics is helpful to an extent, but self-realization should remain as the inspiration for growth. Once you are clear about where you are in the relationship, compared to where you want to be, the goals begin to be established. It is impossible to improve if you continue your effort in a haphazard manner. You must be directed in your actions to allow for a natural, sequential growth and achieve your personal best. As you develop an action plan, it must be specific in the commitment to an acquisition of knowledge, clarifying confusion, overcoming difficulties, and creating a specific schedule of playing and practicing. The clarity of your plans for implementation goes far in providing motivation that supports intent and desire. Once the plan has been clarified, you must be held accountable. Too often you avoid this because of its self-critical nature.

It is human nature to dislike criticism, particularly when you become your own critic, but it is necessary to evaluate and modify the process for ultimate efficiency. You must maintain a positive demeanor throughout the process to overcome disappointments and setbacks. Remember, these moments of frustration are opportunities to acquire a deeper level of awareness. Difficulties along the way of life are what build character. Developing strength of character is at the core of being the best that you can be. The values developed in pursuit of this life force called golf will serve the needs in all aspects of your evolution.

We must maintain self-acceptance in the pursuit of our personal best. Believing we can accomplish at levels beyond the scope of our current capacity is unrealistic. However, we should not accept our weaknesses and do nothing about them. Our willpower is the inner strength enabling us to consistently move forward. The lack of activity and commitment leads to apathy and despair. When activating the will to become our absolute best, motivation is supported and sustained. Willpower overcomes a weakened desire to keep us on course for the achievement of our highest aspiration. The unfailing consistency of purpose and power of the will focuses the intent and supports our efforts as we follow through on the projected plans for ongoing expansion. Now purpose is sustained in achieving our personal best. The course of play remains consistent with the integrity of committed efforts in developing our golfing experience.

Centering

The golf game is a balanced art form within the aesthetic center of our purpose. The game is a mode of existence where its form and content, character and substance, sensibility and rhythms are all part of its wholeness. This emerges from the core of its spiritual connection, to the essence of its character and requirements. The equilibrium created maintains its center of focus. As all capacities within our determined efforts are brought into realized context, we generate an effortless power and accuracy produced by intent. The kinesthetic responses of our body, mind, and spirit unite as we experience the exhilaration from playing the game. We become fully immersed in a focused attention, absorbed in participation, centered on playing capability, as the potential to expand becomes reality.

In remaining centered on the purpose, we are able to elicit mental strength to overcome each limitation and realize a commitment to a course of action. This enables us to develop our playing ability beyond current expectations. As purpose motivates desire, we begin to structure a process that is carefully designed to challenge our ability and bring the intent to the forefront of our pursuit. We gain efficiency as the focal point becomes clearly set on our passion for participation and growth.

When the accomplishment of our current aspiration is realized we establish the next starting point for future goals and objectives. We are now on a journey where the momentum is sustained by its own achievement, recognizing our advancement. As we become energized within the depth of our spiritual development we center at the hub of self-discovery. The game is now rotating around the focused center, balancing efforts, intents, and acceptance of our accomplishments. Now, we must acknowledge the responsibility to organize our journey, setting forth on the achievement of a newly set course focused on the next challenge.

At the center of our golf game are strategic requirements, which progressively reveal themselves as we further understand the complexities of the *it factor*. In the continued development, vision of what we truly want to achieve in our playing should be clear and enjoyable. The goals must be structured in balance with a centered mind-set, intent, desire, time commitment, and physical capabilities. If we do not develop a strategic approach, it becomes impossible for us to create conditions in which to advance without extreme frustration. The grace and ease of play desired will meet with unnecessary interference of our capabilities and will be in danger of being eroded. It becomes imperative to create a carefully organized action plan, complete with a time schedule of various levels of achievability of our desired outcome. We are able to take control of clear sailing to our destination. Our center is supported by proper ballast and stabilized by the ebb and flow of our design. Clarity of precise vision of a course design assures the fulfillment of our desire. It all comes back to the passionate effort to satisfy the deepest, heartfelt yearning between a structured plan and our playing purpose. Human nature, defined within our spirit, is now lifted and realigned on center. A sense of being is in tune with the perfect harmony, with effortless fulfillment in the experience of golf and life.

Self Actualization

Finding one's purpose in golf and in a broader sense life is a very personal and far reaching introspective pursuit. In all endeavors we discover the truths that lie at the core, revealed through the processes we develop to efficiently experience each situation or circumstance. As our course continues to evolve, the ability to respond to our individual needs and desires provides the medium and guiding light that leads us on a path of discovery to a spiritual connection. If we remain open to the potential risks that lie within the adventure, and accept our intuitive reactions to the challenges, then we are presented with the ultimate trophy of a self-actualized life. The exhilaration of our peak moments continually reveal and support a purposeful life. We are playing our game with a deliberate purpose and a passionate pursuit. Perfectly centered and balanced from the process of our actions, we follow our quest with authentic realization from the core of our spiritual essence.

As we become self-actualized golfers, we gain a deeper level of self-awareness. This provides strength of commitment having the power to overcome adversity. Perpetual motion is propelled by an infinite energy source, self-generated in an adventure that we seek and accomplishment that we achieve. We begin to unveil our connection to the quantum realm of the finite experience within an infinite spiritual existence. With an accepting shift in conscious awareness and unrestricted willingness, we are able to expand our understanding of the potential that lies dormant within. A decisive action is realized and the expansion of our capability is supportive of the progress witnessed in our game. The course design becomes fully integrated within the boundaries of expectations as players of the game.

Self-conscious anxiety is diminished, no longer threatened by outside critiques. Freed to take appropriate action, based on the clarity of our well-founded beliefs, we are without any disabling sense of guilt or potential shame and disgrace. We therefore maintain dignity in spite of any misfortune. Now we can remain open to intuitive spontaneity as we are released from inhibitions. Our work becomes play; play becomes our life's work. It is hard to identify which is which. Moving through a course of play with a graceful ease of motion, should only be defined by acceptance of the experience. Thoughts and impulses are only ours, they are not infringed upon by conventional requirements of outwardly, imposed regulation. The standard of play comes from within the oneness of who we are and what we accept to be true.

When we become inwardly directed, we are refreshed with an understanding that creates our own source of inspiration. However, we are also inspired through a higher, more vital, spiritual essence that flows through the quantum realm of all that is. The connectedness to this outer space that surrounds us helps us understand a worldly experience. Creative instincts are free to wander and discover for themselves with the realization of the inborn potentiality leading to the ultimate achievement in golf and life. As we become more self-actualized, we are able to let go of the preconceived notion of what may or may not be possible and expand a vision of the future from a higher point of view. The constant rejuvenation of energy in our life force is released with unrestricted enthusiasm as we continue the journey we have charted.

Arrival for Departure

An ongoing acceptance of our potential for the desired outcome of our golfing experience runs true and passionate, like the playful nature lying within our life force. We discover wondrous revelations and insights into our own character when we create and play our game without trying to over emphasize the growth process. Evolution becomes a result of and not the purpose for the continuation of our deliberate efforts, as we plan and discover a true course of action. Our course design is created in the blending of passion and purpose instilled in our individuality with an acceptance of the discoveries along the way. How we cope with challenges opens the opportunities during our journey. Rewards are recognized by the sense of satisfaction, through a spirit-based accomplishment, graciously accepted within the humility of a divine nature. All of the components of a well-planned game are provided with endless enjoyment through the many cycles of playful participation. Each round of golf opens the potential for a new and wondrous journey within the unrestricted nature of our design. Process and pursuit are supported by the intensity of passion and the clarity of purpose.

Setting a course with an authentic, personal design based on awakened intrinsic values, our nature is defined by cooperative melding within the game's requirements. We understand that this game, which we have the privilege to be part of, is truly more than just a recreational pastime. It is an adventure that continually challenges us and supports our personal vision. As we overcome self-doubt, and feel the exhilaration of accomplishment, we are provided with the hope and anticipation associated with each ball strike. The handicaps we place upon ourselves are overcome as we learn to be totally committed to and immersed in the aura of the game. Our character is structurally supported by the passion lying within the cornerstone of the course design. The secrets of the game unfold and unconditional acceptance of ease and grace is experienced in our play. This allows for a holistic connection to the *why* and allows mind, body, and spirit to become one with the game. We are now playing from the depths of our being, to the outer limits of our expanding ability. The search continues for the authentic acceptance of our relationship to the game. A sincere recognition of the successes along the path reaffirms our intent. Unlocking ability, we expand beyond any limits of conscious awareness and accept life's lessons.

We become conditioned with a peaceful acceptance of the golf process. As our minds expand our conscious awareness becomes non-controlling and we gain a relaxed, playful nature. We attain clarity within our conditional feeling, opening a response to the natural swing. We are now able to *go fore it* without the pressure of any artificial desire to control. Now, we experience the course that dreams are made of. As we refocus intent, and clear the way for our total commitment we are stimulated by and immersed in an optimal energy source.

With the realization of courage and confidence that is well supported, we can take on any challenge without anticipation of potential failure. The thinking process is elevated, but also stabilized with an acceptance, of an inner poise that is enhanced and supported by a spiritual connection.

Our course of action is well designed, allowing us to accept the best of what we have to offer. When we find a center, an inner desire to achieve a self-actualized commitment allows for an infinite journey. When we arrive, we find ourselves fully equipped, ready for departure to the next level of existence. Passion brings us complete understanding of the purpose, exemplifying our pursuit of the game. We move toward clarification of the processes often created to carry out the pursuit through our purposeful play. As we journey forward on a course set by the highest aspirations for successful outcome, our best efforts fulfill our expectations. Self-actualization becomes centered. Arriving now at the next door of opportunity we unlock and open ourselves for the newly discovered challenges that allows us to once again depart into the unknown realm of future existence.

Part Three

The Process

There are times in our lives when we become captivated by a compelling force that creates an interest or attracts us to an activity. We are stimulated by a passion to participate. As curiosity peaks our interest, we begin a process of discovery that raises a higher awareness and attraction to its power. Motivation translates into a connection with a purposeful involvement. The desire to pursue the requirements necessary for successful achievement presents a need for a specific process of continued exploration. In order to accomplish anything worthwhile in life, we must accept the responsibility to develop a specific, structured procedure where we either create for ourselves, or adopt from a pre-existing methodology. Whichever path we chose, the journey requires a clear vision of what we ultimately wish to accomplish.

There must be a deep sense of determination and unfailing commitment to support the desire and fully realize the goals. Beyond our own abilities developed through well structured learning, we must also connect to a spiritual essence that lies within the universal force of its existence. Once we connect to this force, we recognize our fundamental purpose. Having a strong passion and purpose provides the energy for us to achieve our goals; having a process provides the means. As we begin to understand the inner workings of the mind, we open ourselves to the forces within a spiritual makeup, eliciting the timeless, universal law of attraction. This powerful force activates an unfolding of our responsive acceptance to all that we encounter. We are now freed to pursue our aspired goals with effortless action. This realization should be carried over and be applied to all of our endeavors, as the search continues for a fully realized experience. My desire is to provide an understandable process that supports the nature of a positive golf experience. We are then provided with a guidance system for the passionate pursuit of our achievable goals and objectives.

Our process will become an integral part of who we are and how we conduct ourselves. The methods we use provide the strength of conviction as confidence grows. The belief in our ability is essential for success in all endeavors. We develop a competitive edge free of the ego's false portrayals. Commitment to the process supports our purpose and allows for an effortless pursuit. Passionate involvement is maintained. A self-actualized, authentic life is the result.

We should exercise patience in our development, while maintaining an unfailing, faithful execution of every stroke and search to manifest the law of attraction's power. If we examine our moments of incompetence and disappointment, we discover that we were not fully accepting the positive expectation of outcome necessary for success.

Chapter Eleven

Law of Attraction

Heart's Desire

During my early, formative years of playing and practicing golf, I was immersed and totally consumed by what I thought, at that time, was my destiny. Not unlike many others, all I dreamed about was my future on the PGA Tour. Each day, from early April to the end of October, my heart and soul were overtaken by the enormous satisfaction I felt as I pursed my passion. The competition and camaraderie brought me significant pleasure. As I matured, expanding my playing exposure, the desire for competing began to dissipate. There was something about the importance of competing, both in winning, and losing that no longer made sense. I realized that my desire to pursue the finer aspects of the game began to intensify. Although my heart was no longer inspired by the competitive aspect of playing, my deepest purpose shifted to a new reality, opening my spirit to a more connected, elevated reason for the pursuit. ,

The majestic nature of golf, a truly, remarkable sport, captivated my imagination and I began discovering what *it* is about golf that transcends the final score. The spiritual sense of the game inspired me to begin an enduring search for the deeper meaning of life and its relationship to the nature of my game. I have been led down a path, and find myself in a totally involved commitment, sharing my feelings and knowledge with as many people as possible. My passion has never been stronger and the purpose has never been clearer. Now, the process has become part of me, reaching new levels of efficiency and dedication. I can only hope that the ongoing intensity of the pursuit, coupled with the strength of my unfailing efforts establishes a legacy that will live on. I am blessed to share what this game has given to me and pay it forward. The process now supports passion and frees my heart's desire in the pursuit of a true pre-destined purpose.

We are all here on Earth as individual miracles of the creative manifestation of a divine, spiritual essence that is one with all of existence. As we begin to witness the miracles of our individual life force, we come to understand the infinite potential energy source waiting to release its flow, and move us to new levels of involvement. This heartfelt determination lifts us out of an apathetic, mundane existence and gives us unstoppable momentum, which, once set in motion, cannot be halted by any outside force. We overcome inertia, power our ambition with perpetual motion, and live with unrestrained enthusiasm.

Now we begin accepting the game as a living experience, whose challenges and obstacles are nothing more than a microcosm of everyday existence. Then, the game will reveal the answers to many of life's questions, that at times seem so overwhelming. Regardless of how our game unfolds the next round presents a new opportunity for exhilaration, promising hope that lies within its divine nature. Faith becomes unyielding as we play through any obstacles that stand in our way. Our heart's desire is strengthened through effort and passionate purpose, a reflection of our life along the pursuit's chosen way.

Life Response

We all carry within us a remarkable power, with an attractive magnetism that, when properly focused, brings into each life whatever it is that we desire to improve our condition. If intentions are clear, just, and aligned properly with the universal spirit of goodness, then our thoughts will manifest the path. We perceive the desired result by remaining open-minded and connected to our sensibilities.

Much of the indecisiveness that we experience in our golf game comes from a lack of total belief and commitment. In order to become fully connected to the requirements of play, we must focus on a type of thoughtful structure that accepts the probability of ultimate achievement. If the possibility of a negative outcome enters into the mind's eye, we risk disaster. As we realize the potential to willfully execute and achieve the desired result, we begin to accept the possibility for a successful outcome. A life response takes control and we are connected to a spirit-centered belief that bypasses our intellectual interference. Our mind is now quiet and accepting. We no longer need to waste moments deliberating possible results. The mode of play is graceful, free from fear and anxiety that bring stressful experiences. Self-doubts are replaced with absolute expectation of positive results as we let go and allow the divinity within our spiritual essence infiltrate our awareness. The secret to successful achievement in golf and life reveals itself in unsuspecting ways. The unattainable is not only possible, but at certain creative moments is probable. We are able to achieve our best expectations through totally effortless motion.

When we open up to the potential of this guidance system, we are inspired and internalize a freedom in our existence. The feelings of elation fill our spirit, providing momentum within an enthusiastic ability to overcome resistance and fully accept an inner potential. Yes, we can! However, if we are to take full advantage of this seemingly mystical law, we must be willing to work on conscious commitment, pursuing thought processes that are open to our ultimate achievement. Constantly installing mental thoughts that align with clear, concise goals requires practice. Through the use of visualization and affirmation, we gain a controlling power to affect positive outcome. As our efforts are realized, we must gratefully accept the results, while avoiding any potential negative interference.

We should exercise patience in our development, while maintaining an unfailing, faithful execution of every stroke and search to manifest the law of attraction's power. If we examine our moments of incompetence and disappointment, we discover that we were not fully accepting the positive expectation of outcome necessary for success. However, if we continually recognize the belief of our desired, potential expectation, then we are able to elicit the life response lying within the law of attraction. In my teaching process I often refer to the method of acquiring knowledge as the "learning continuum." This continuum says that if we can conceive *it* through our intellect and perceive *it* in all of our senses; we will open an ability to achieve *it* using a kinesthetic connection. Soon, we begin to believe *it* within our spiritual acceptance. Confidence grows as we receive *it* through expectations of positive outcome. Periodically, we are out of focus, apathetic, or we slip into a state where we deceive *it*. At that time, we must be able to reach deep within ourselves to retrieve *it*. Now, we must go back to the beginning and re-establish our understanding of the basic concept, as we conceive *it* once again. Each time we travel through this "continuum of learning" we are able to achieve a higher level of ownership of our ability.

Inner Freedom

Our world bombards us with an overabundance of stimulus, both positive and negative. This continually places our minds in motion with a massive amount of thought provoking activity, most of which is useless. Typically this adds nothing for our overall well-being, but it still exists. We have all had the experience of an image or thought that we cannot eliminate from our consciousness. It keeps us awake at night. If we examine these thoughts, we find that most of them had no long-lasting effect on any outcome in our lives. However, upon applying this understanding of mental activity, we realize how this invades our thoughts on the golf course as we experience the trials and tribulations of the game. Success comes down to the ability to set up goals and deal with the conditions for a positive life response, while contemplating our desired accomplishment. The responsibility lies directly on our shoulders. We must find a path to follow that puts us in connection with positive frames of reference.

Whatever we expose ourselves to dictates who we develop into. If we are to become masters of our game, we first must become masters of our minds. Filtration of thoughts is the key to the positive programming that is so critical to ultimate achievement in life. Seeking out positive input continually feeds constructive focus and our inner mind begins to accept beliefs that produce inner freedom from negative influences. Choices are strengthened by a fundamental acceptance of the values that lie within the cornerstone of our support structure. Secondary choices remain in alignment with and supported by the strength of our desired outcome. The bottom line is that positive feedback and results emerge if our mind is freed from negative input producing undesirable results. Now, our inner freedom supports the positive life response as it casts its magical spell through the law of attraction.

The fertile ground for growth is tilled, depending upon each life response and how we set our minds in motion. We realize that the law of attraction is not so mystical after all. No more so than the miracle of the growth and bloom of the sunflower as it follows the source of energy through its life span. Also we have the ability to elevate our game to a level of acceptance using our energy source. This frees our inner mind from worry, fear, anxiety, and control while it opens us to the universal source of our spiritual guidance.

As we become progressively aware of the higher realizations available to us through our freedom of thought, we will find that our true *response ability* does not need to be imposed upon by outside sources. We are now able to make our own judgments through intuitive sensibility. Outside stimulus does not penetrate subconscious programming unless we decide to welcome it in. Our belief systems are constructed by us, for us, and because of us without fear or doubt. Inner freedom allows surety of commitment in every stroke we make and carries over to the well conceived actions we take from the golf course. We experience a life of effortless thriving. Creative thinking is limitless and opens the directional force at the core of our passion. Inner freedom awakens an unfailing purpose to an ongoing process of evolution, leading us hole by hole, stroke by stroke, on a chosen course as our destiny is revealed. The final score becomes an honest record of the self-actualized construct we experience in the game's reflection in our lives.

Universal Connectedness

My first introduction to the wonders of golf at age six was the compelling force that motivated me to write this book. My ongoing inquiry into the *how* of the game has progressively led me to the deeper meaning of the life force that lies within the *why* of the game. As my golfing experience has continued to reveal its secrets, I have come to understand that within the content of its finite nature a connection exists to the infinite aspect of all that is. There seems to be a universal, cosmic interaction that when examined from a more distant perspective reveals a point of view that can be learned and applied. This has helped me uncover a better understanding of who I am and how I fit into the inter-connected cosmos of infinite existence.

The search for meaning and fulfillment is broken down into the relationship between our self-centered ego and divine nature, which are both connected to a higher purpose. When comprehension of our individual nature transcends a perceived duality that we have been conditioned to believe, we reach a balance. Then, we become the part of our game in golf and life that penetrates the spiritual essence of our heart and soul. As capabilities improve, our beliefs unfold in the development of a full awareness within the principles of life. Typically these are deeply hidden beneath the illusion of separateness. The universal intelligence is released and the inferiority of ego centered existence is dismissed. We begin to acquire the ability to understand that our life force provides the necessary responses to the situations encountered. At that point, we play a game that appropriately reveals the creative, intuitive responses to our need. As these are released spontaneously through a divine guidance, we accept our *response ability* in a trusting fashion. The fallacy of our ego centered ability to control every shot in life becomes a new revelation. This allows for a life response arising naturally, not hindered by any aspect of self-doubt. Continuing to allow the presence of a universal connection in our play, we are surprised and elated by our accomplishments. As our connection progresses we are able to remove the uncertainty and attain a sense of security that allows for an unrestricted flow of execution. This results in levels of achievement that we never thought possible. The *if onlys* and *perhaps maybes* in our game play are replaced by the capacity to deal with our encounters. A surety of outcome is empowered and energizes an effortless acceptance of the law of attraction.

With a revival of innate ability to take on the challenges of growth and expansion, the pleasures of play are experienced as they are truly meant to be. When we free ourselves from the controlling desires for the final score, our play is liberated from all fear of failure through a life response as the results are gracefully accepted. In a fully realized game there is no failure, there is only a well-supported guidance of continual experience.

From this moment on I suggest that you experience golf and life with this deep sense of connectedness. Accept the guidance systems of the spiritual force that comes to you through your conscious thoughts. Keep those that inspire your intents and desires as you expand the spirit of your being. This ability will mark the acceptance of your life response at the core of the law of attraction.

Gracious Acceptance

The relativity between the fundamental aspect of participation in golf and the divine nature at the core of our humanness must now be considered to graciously accept the probability of the law of attraction. In order to further understand the power of the attractive forces that provide everything positive and desired, we first need to understand the phenomenon from the scientific perspective. Everything within our universal sphere of reference, at its least common denominator, is nothing more than a mass of atoms and subatomic particles in constant motion. The words that I have laid down are ink on paper made up of a basic molecular construction. The entire format of our world shares this same composition. The thoughts and concepts that I am suggesting come from a culmination of energies over a lifetime of experiences, attracting me through my intent, desire, and pursuit. It all comes down to a positive flow of energy that is emitted one to another. As you read these words you are resonating within your molecular structure while you accept, reject, ponder, and contemplate the concepts that have their own vibrating force. Your experience with the game starts with a thought that you attract for unclear reasons. Many times these experiences are simply explained away as happenstance or coincidence. However, when we look back on our past and take time to analyze our lives, there are no coincidences, only a life journey of experiences that historically appear predestined and connected to a cosmic master plan of cause and effect. The directions we choose to take dictate what we become through the experiences that we encounter.

The vibration and resonance of all thoughts and emotions, either positive or negative, release a magnetic attraction which controls the outcome of our play. The results of the scores in life are directly correlated with how we allow our minds to be programmed. At times, we need to have a defensive energy shield in place and at other moments of acceptance; we must allow this force field to open, regardless of the impending vulnerability. Our decisions and choices are what we allow into our lives as we all have a power to manifest our destiny.

When we have been blessed it is of utmost importance to be grateful for all that has come our way. We must be careful, however, not to focus our thoughts on what we don't want. The negative thoughts create the same type of magnetic force that attracts the undesired outcome. The classic example on the golf course is when we are required to hit a shot across water. I have often heard a playing partner express, "Water is like a magnet, which seems to attract my golf ball!" The splash is witnessed as the fate is sealed. The resistance that a situation presents is exactly what brings on the disaster. Instead, we need a grateful acceptance of the situation as we are confronted and attract a positive outcome. So, consider appreciating the challenging situations, on and off the golf course, as you learn to accept the potential for a positive outcome. These are the true opportunistic moments that connect human experience to our heart's desire. Our life response continues to provide the inner freedom supplied by the magnetic forces carried out through the law of attraction. Understanding and believing in this law assures the process to be carried out with our most sincere intensions. When our life response aligns with our heart's desire we achieve an inner sense of freedom and expectation through the law of attraction.

The sanctuary of the golf course focuses the connection to a spirituality that eases the control of the subconscious mind. It is here with the depth of awareness of challenge and opportunity that a detachment from fear of failure is established.

Chapter Twelve

The Meditative Mind

Sacred Space

Understanding the power of the law of attraction allows for an acceptance of the many occurrences that seem to appear just at the time when they are needed the most. As a trusting mind-set becomes able to transcend the limitations of a desire to manipulate the outcome of situations and circumstances, a mental certainty is opened to a relaxation response. When a freedom of flow is discovered, the deeper reaches of an intuitive sensibility is penetrated. A self-determined, liberated attitude accepts the strength of commitment that produces a trusting capability. Rounds of golf can take on a more meaningful experience by tapping into the spiritual connection to faith in the capacity to carry out the requirements of every stroke played. A golf experience is now achieved that joins the sacred space of the course of play with the intuitive spirit of a meditative mind-set. A realization of what *it* is all about is becoming internalized. Inspired by an accumulation of experience, a strong belief system begins to emerge. Our sense ability is energized by an excitement and enthusiasm that releases the playful child that resides within our spiritual being.

Inside this mental state of youthful enthusiasm and exuberance lies a vast openness. The sanctuary of the golf course focuses the connection to a spirituality that eases the control of the subconscious mind. It is here with the depth of awareness of challenge and opportunity that a detachment from fear of failure is established. Inner poise is internalized, as a non-controlling, thinking process is engaged. Thoughts that may produce destructive penetrating circumstantial results must be silenced. Protection against the emotional reactions that adversely affect intent moves the spirit above the frustrations and disappointments that are sure to occur. A tranquil state of well-being is accepted and trusted. It is only then that the innate strength of commitment secures the centered structure of our playing capacity.

When we gain the ability to accept the truth within a spiritual connection, we begin to realize that our physical bodies are just the structural support that carries out a willful intent. As we look inside, we find a special place which elicits the change of attitude and achieves the *response ability* to our game. Now we are able to accept and overcome the challenge of each stroke. We are freed from psychological deficiencies when we transform our thoughts from the burden of control to a more spiritual acceptance of results. Learning to pay attention to our instinctive reaction we achieve our ultimate potential and receive satisfaction with the effort brought forth.

Opening the pathway to the sacred space within unlocks the secrets of the game. Our soulful nature is liberated and provided with an enduring ability to achieve the consistency of progress. We assess this ability through different methods of constructive, mental programming. The mind is capable of so much more than we even imagine. When we eliminate the interference of our limiting beliefs we prevent our past condition from imposing upon us. We must de-program before we can re-program. This inner sensibility referred to is the direct contact point with our spiritual center. Although intangible, this space has absolute control over our *play ability*. We must start a process of decontamination of the degenerative beliefs that may infiltrate the core of our self-realization. Spirituality can then be set in motion with infinite strength. Our sacred space is completely cleansed and we elicit a place of peaceful retreat, immersing ourselves within the wisdom of past experience. We capture the wholeness of our total involvement of mind, body, and spirit.

Relaxation Response

Our game is constantly challenged by an ability to remain focused on the task at hand. Fleeting thoughts continue to bombard us, disrupting our process in the course of play. The intrinsic beauty of golf lies within the multitude of variables that confront us as our game unfolds. Each situation requires us to thoroughly analyze its nature, narrow down the choices of appropriate action, and decide on the proper procedure. We settle into an acceptance of our decision, to clear the mind as we focus on the requirement of the moment, and execute the shot. To achieve this, we cannot be in a state of fear, worry, or anxiety. These emotions might detach us from the necessary, intuitive connection with our natural ability to carry out the proper stroke. Just prior to execution, we must put all of our preparation to work and slip into a calm acceptance within our mind-set. Then we can find the assurance of a relaxation response in the meditative moment of contact. This is the first stage in a process with which most people are familiar.

We usually visualize how we want to achieve our desired result, analyze a problem at some level, and attempt to execute the shot. However, the procedure itself might bring on its own infiltrated tension during the actual stroke. All of our ability to intellectualize the necessities for successful outcome must somehow give way to our capability to calm the mind and activate our intuitive nature. Now, our intent carries out the process in a confident, peaceful pursuit. Our mind-set achieves a relaxed state of poised readiness, removed from all distracting thoughts. The final point of creative, focused, attention opens us to the decisive, split second execution so necessary for optimal levels of achievement. This is what separates the good player from those with exceptional capability.

We are now ready to take our game to a new level of understanding and achievement as we become true students of the game. The unfolding of our process reveals a methodology lifting us out of the fog, casting a clarity of connection between our mind, body, and spirit. Awareness, stemming from the depth of instinct, encompasses and controls our actions. We become completely carefree, but this spontaneity is not out of desperation. Instead, we have reached within ourselves by focusing our creative awareness that exists in the trust and faith of pure acceptance.

This opens our mind to the possibility of the ultimate achievement that we desire. Now we accept the probability of a successful outcome. We are able to fully transcend any preconceived negative beliefs that may be lingering. Thoughts of failure are not even a remote possibility. Our very nature is maturing to a level of unfailing commitment. This allows us to accept all that we become both on and off the chosen course of our personal design.

As we become conscious of our ability to expand awareness, we liberate the mind from the boundaries of the course we choose to play. Nothing that exists in the creative process imposes a limitation on our pursuits, as long as it is structured around the expectation of a positive outcome. We are carried by the momentum of continued achievement. Inertia propels us forward effortlessly, as our game continues to cast its reflection on the unending realization of the true desires with a responsive, achievable outcome.

Imagine That

The mind has been proven to be far more powerful than our superficial understanding of what it easily accepts. It is not surprising that research is ongoing in realizing the power of positive affirmations and their resulting consequences. Many of the disease treatment hospitals and recovery centers are now successfully using visualization techniques to control and cure diseases. In some cases medical intervention through traditional methodology has not been successful, yet some patients have had miraculous, positive results. For centuries, most of the Eastern philosophies have valued a heightened awareness and comprehension of the powers of the mind, far superior to our accepted usage in the West. In athletic endeavors we are seeing some of our top athletes utilizing visualization techniques prior to their competition to gain a higher awareness thus increasing their abilities. Many times applying this ability to control their mind allows them to even overcome the discomfort of painful injuries, which could otherwise sideline players unfamiliar with these practices.

We are often more efficient in our pursuits when we tap into the power of our imagination. This can lead us in directions of our pursuit with an increased efficiency. The process of focused attention and the ability to visualize a plan of decisive action empowers us to overcome any level of self-doubt and assure a more consistent result. This imaginative power has the potential to provide us with a world of perspective on situations having a dramatic effect on the achievability of our desired intent. Imagining an outcome before the actual effort has an amazing affect on the consistency of a reasonable, predictable result. We then overcome negative impulses of possible disasters.

Daydreaming is a good example of how our imagination removes us from a stressful situation and places us in a chosen space that provides relief from our current situation. This activity is beneficial as it produces an escape from where we are and transports us to a peaceful retreat. This enables us to recover, clear our minds, while allowing us to establish our ability to continue our pursuit.

In the game of golf these mental abilities are being explored constantly by the top competitors. Their focused attention, coupled with a peace of mind, must be in perfect balance if they are not to succumb to an impulsive response to decisive action. The conscious and subconscious minds must be in complete, relaxed agreement. Only then can they maintain the poised flow of body movement that releases congruent sensibility of consistent ball striking. The achievement of the connection of mind, body, and spirit to the *it factor* lies within the *response ability* to the game.

Activating our imagination is a natural phenomenon, although most of us are not consciously aware of it. We have a constant series of thoughts flowing through our minds that trigger ideas, many of which are dismissed. We need to capture the most useful of those thoughts that support our potential for continued growth. We too often reject the most powerful life changing possibilities because of a lack of faith. The most creative thoughts are the birth of genius that comes from our universal connectiveness to the divine guidance that is at the heart of the law of attraction. When a great idea materializes, we should not reject it for fear of ridicule or criticism. These magical moments of creative impulse have been provided to us for a reason. We must have faith to follow through in an accepting manner if our process is to maintain an inspired motivation. The mind must remain open to the flow of imagination if we are to realize our full potential. Purposeful efforts now have the inspiration that continues to maintain a passionate involvement, allowing for an ever expanding process that supports the pursuit.

Hypnotic Trance

Our ability to elicit a point of focused attention eliminates the conscious mind from interfering with an intuitive, kinesthetic response. The natural movement of the body lies within our ability to achieve the desired state of mindful mindlessness. This moment of truth must be captured in a relaxation response that is deliberately triggered by some method of distraction from the requirements of the task. It is distinctly different from the concentration required in the preparation for playing the stroke. This meditative moment is more of a hypnotic event which allows the fluid motion to be released in the natural swing that we rehearsed on the practice tee. Most shots missed on the course are the result of a last moment mental impulse to overreact by exerting additional energy to control our desired result. The conscious impulse to deliberately manipulate the ball often affects our intended effort to achieve a positive outcome. We must learn to allow the ball to be hit, rather than trying to hit the ball. This is the secret of consistent ball striking.

How then can we train our minds to come to this relaxed mind-set at the moment of impact? Let us consider the nature of this state of mind that some might refer to as a hypnotic trance. Many of us consider hypnosis with an attitude of doubt as to whether it is possible to achieve this level of momentary disassociation with reality. We consciously believe that we must be in total control if we are to actively achieve our purpose. As I work with my students, in an effort to bring them into alignment with the trusting of their natural swing, I have found a variety of methods to help them discover their individual relaxation response. The purpose of this process is to clearly determine the necessity of clear thought in their ball striking consistency. We must accept that the hypnotic moment of truth should be consistently adhered to.

Most students, over the years, admit to periodic vacancies in their conscious minds. This is merely a wandering that we refer to as absent mindedness that is very disengaging from our intent. We must maintain a connection with our subconscious where our creative instinct lives.

During these times of mental wandering, our minds disconnect from a congruent balance with our body and spirit. This disrupts the desired level of blissful peace and quiet. Often those who have experienced this state learn to deliberately nurture an ability to remain focused. A conditioned acceptance of positive results has a dramatic effect on a consistency of outcome. If we learn to acquire this state of mind-set, we can deliberately use it in our day-to-day activities.

An experience that most people realize and will admit to occurs when they are driving in the car. Even though they are in complete control of the vehicle, they are less than conscious of what it takes to keep the car on the road. At times, passages of roadway go by and they suddenly realize that they had no recollection of what just transpired. They come back to consciousness only to realize that they just passed their exit. How could this possibly happen? Well, our mind has become so comfortable and accepting that it allows our bodies to react appropriately by keeping the car on the highway in a state of peaceful retreat. In applying this to the game of golf, we reach the depths of our subconscious through deliberate processes, such as the recollection of a previous successful outcome. Through the repetition of proper swing mechanics, during practice sessions, the expectation of solid ball striking becomes engrained in the meditative mind-set of acceptance.

Meditative Mind-set

As we delve deeper into what *it* is that the game of golf offers in *its* requirements to play in a skillful manner, we learn to successfully control our thought processes. The world we live in today fills the mind with tension and anxiety produced by the uncertainty of our times. The game of golf should provide us with an escape to a place of comfort and relaxation. Hopefully, we are beginning to realize that proper, consistent ball striking requires a focused mind that eliminates any distractions. For us to be able to achieve this state of being we need to exercise our mental capacity. By eliciting a sense of calm tranquility at the moment of impact we achieve a total acceptance of an alignment in the mind, body, spirit connection. We might take a page out of the pro's playbook and develop a strong commitment to daily meditation to achieve this capability.

Meditation has mixed reactions to Western ways of thinking. We tend to believe that meditation can cause our mind to lose control of our conscious thoughts. Instead, it expands our capability to accept a heightened level of subconscious acceptance that prepares us for higher levels of accomplishment. Learning to meditate enhances not only our capability in golf, but also all aspects of life's experience. Many of the suggestions that have been examined thus far have expressed the need to lose control of the wanting desire and adhere to a clarity of intent. Our potential to open the possibility for consistent outcome is now achieved. This helps us to find the peaceful, inner acceptance to trust our faithful efforts.

Through the practice of daily meditation our mind achieves a positive relaxation state, whenever it is required. The process of meditation progressively removes the stressful thoughts from the reality of your immediate environment that contains negative distractions. Our metabolism is dramatically affected by the meditative process that provides a cleansing of toxic thinking. Mental and physical well-being is also protected from the destructive intrusion of negative programming. This has been proven to have significant healing capabilities and is now beginning to work its way into the mainstream of conventional medicine. Although you might initially resist the meditative process, I highly recommend that you commit yourself to fifteen minutes per day, for one week, to accomplish this meditative state. Simply sit in a comfortable, relaxed position and focus on your breathing as you release the thoughts from your mind. At first, keep it simple. Do not look for immediate success and do not attempt to control the outcome. A peaceful mind-set comes with patience and perseverance.

As you achieve the blissful place within your mind you find yourself making fewer errors, having better judgment, and making more comprehensive decisions. Your patience and tolerance improves. As you become able to put your mind at peace, you will also begin to enjoy a calm, joyous, and powerful focus. Opening to the vastness of infinite potentiality, while patiently progressing with a level of expectation, supports the perseverance promoting your newly found capabilities.

The journey into the world of the meditative mind-set quiets the conscious mind to reveal the inner self and provide relief from the dominance of the ego. Now, a self-realized player emerges in all endeavors, with an ease and grace of accomplishment. Connecting with an acceptance of efforts, without interference, allows the spiritual connection of being in the game. Playing in total recognition and realization of a relaxation response engages a focused attention in the meditative moment of contact.

This awareness allows us to move the spirit of our game play and achieve an enlightened understanding of the purpose of each stroke in life. Our process is now established with a clarity of force that dismisses the negative impulses lying dormant within the mental gremlins of the mind.

Chapter Thirteen

Thoughtful Connections

Duality Within

Our brains are complex thinking machines. If left to their own devices, they lead us to an unbalanced understanding of the actions and decisions we should make. The experiences we have impact how we direct our thoughts, emotions, impulses, attitudes, feelings, and the responses to the situations that we encounter both on and off the golf course. If we react with a *response ability* to our situation, we must become aware of the thinking process that creates the most efficiency in the decisive actions that affect the outcome of our play.

There are universally used expressions that have been passed down as a means of identifying some of the malfunctions that affect our thinking. At certain times we are lured into states of apathetic or non-focused attitudes and experience dramatic, unexpected consequences. As a result, we openly remark "what was I thinking" or "where was my brain." Also, we may follow a bad round of golf with an exclamation like, "I have half a mind to give up this game." Where do these statements come from? If we heighten our understanding of how our brain functions and what *it* is that affects the affirmative action that we chose to take, then we are able to command more control of our situation in a fully mindful state of being.

Our understanding of brain functions has expanded dramatically over the past thirty years. It is clearly accepted that the right and left hemispheres process and interpret information in different ways. The left hemisphere is responsible for linear, logical, verbal, reality-based, analytical processing. The left hemisphere of the brain is very tuned in to the requirements of the moment. Creativity is fostered in the right hemisphere, holistic in its comprehension and capable of random processing. It relies on a more symbolic, intuitive, and imaginative orientation in its interpretative ability. This hemisphere utilizes non-verbal, analytical capabilities that see the big picture, while the left hemisphere picks the information apart. As golfers, it is important that we develop an ability to utilize both hemispheres in a cooperative agreement in order to accomplish what it takes to become a wholly realized player. Second guessing is eliminated once the hemispheres come into congruent alignment and a decisive action is accepted.

The game of golf requires the usage and balance of both hemispheres. Care must be taken to work toward the hemispheric integration in a cooperative alignment. This allows our sensibility to develop wholeness in our efforts to carry out the requirements of play. As we apply the knowledge and understanding of this hemispheric specialization, we direct the congruent agreement of the half-truths that exist in each side of our mind that leads to our decisive actions. We need to learn to connect the messages that are sent to us from the two hemispheres. Our responses are guided by the input being considered as we formulate our final decision and allow our abilities to be realized. Once the decision is made our brain is put into a restful, submissive state of agreement. Now, we have complete commitment in full cooperation from both sides of our mind. No second guessing is necessary.

Balanced Brain

The battle that goes on between the two hemispheres of the brain is continuous and must be dealt with directly to gain the consistency that we seek. First, however, we have to discover the significance of what each hemisphere has to offer. The very nature of the specialization within the two hemispheres is what the intriguing nature of our sport requires if we are to progress from one level to the next. With a better understanding of the specialization of hemispheric brain function, we accept the necessity of studying the physical requirements of specific fundamental methodologies and techniques. These must be learned on an intellectual level and calls on the capacity for cognitive comprehension to be installed within the lobes of the left hemisphere. If, however, the mechanical aspect of our game play were to be left unchecked, we would be functioning in a completely robotic manner. We would be no better than Iron Byron, the golf ball testing robot that has been utilized by the United States Golf Association at their headquarters in Far Hills, New Jersey. This machine could be precisely set to hit perfect golf shots. It could not, however, react emotionally with elation or disappointment to the results, nor could it respond to the requirements of intuitive sensibility so necessary for creative play. There lies the demand for right hemispheric intervention. Our potential is achieved in the holistic expression that supports the magical *it factor* of this game, while stimulating a passionate pursuit. Support of our purpose relies on the ability to tap both hemispheres for what they have to offer.

As we begin to comprehend the complex nature of the game, our minds become scattered. We must learn to stay sharply focused on the precision of the fundamentals for proper execution of the stroke. The left brain's capability is critical for our analytical mind to deal with the physical process of swinging a club in a variety of different technical procedures. Our two hemispheres should adapt to the configuration of circumstance, which calls for a certain stroke to be played. This analytical ability to meet the momentary needs through a learned, precise response of body mechanics and shot configuration becomes ingrained within the left hemisphere. These stored thoughts are called up at any time to apply to the necessities of the moment.

In our golfing experience, however, we are called upon to react in a sensitive manner to a multitude of conditions and situations that require an interpretive ability. This is derived from the deeper understanding of requirements that are only supplied by our right brain. It is reactionary in the requirements of sensibility that our intellectual analysis is not capable of handling. Judgments are challenged based on our circumstance and must be acted upon instantly in an instinctive manner. The message of the physical requirement provided by the left brain's programmed stroke process is then released in a kinesthetic response of intense force. The sense perception is based on the right hemisphere's instinctive analysis. If we avoid last minute indecisiveness, the action created by the interrelationship of the two hemispheres comes into agreement on the requirements of the stroke to be played. We learn to progressively acquire an experience in our course of play that is freed from a self-imposed, ego driven desire to live up to artificial perception of achievement. If we simply allow ourselves to have an honest interaction that penetrates the spiritual essence of how we play the game, then we are able to open the pathways for a process to be accepted. The ongoing pursuit is now one of a holistic content and the mind achieves a peaceful joy found in the true power of our play.

Subconscious Resistance

Only when the relationship between the left and right hemispheres are in a cooperative harmony can we expect the free-flowing, confident execution of our desired stroke. When our mind is troubled, one side maintains a controlling dominance, which creates a distrusting mind-set. This results in a defensive mental posture. We are now being consumed by the fear of failure. In this state of mind it becomes difficult, if not impossible, to execute the shot with any level of conviction. Our subconscious sensibility sends out signals of distrust to the nervous system originating from a lack of belief in the possibility of success. The conscious mind then picks up on these signals and quickly recalls past failures. These thoughts have a traumatic effect as we anticipate a reoccurrence of negative outcomes. We have a strong possibility at this point of repeating the feared outcome to the level of precise replication. Even if we are highly motivated to avoid repeating the failed effort, our thought of not wanting a certain outcome is exactly what will materialize.

If we learn to adopt a patient, acceptance of periodic failure, expecting to overcome the subconscious traumatic warning, we reduce the suppressing anxiety of the moment. The acceptance of the possibility of trauma removes us from the path of protective avoidance of pain and releases a believable commitment that allows for a successful effort. Spawned by the strength and power of our willful desire we can overcome the negative influence of previous disasters. These past experiences no longer have the power to override the positive outlook instilled in our current perception. When we restructure our thinking to be more open to new experiences and continue to focus on the positive outcome, our potential has a chance of being realized. Then, we continue the development of positive affirmations and acquire the ability to visualize as we come to expect positive results.

Our subconscious mind does not possess discretionary judgment on what to let in and what to keep out. It is, therefore, continually storing both positive and negative suggestions. It just takes in whatever it is exposed to, combining emotional reaction with past experience, and establishes absolute truths. To alter the mind's perception of current reality, we must find ways to reprogram it. This is where ongoing rehearsal comes in. On the practice tee we are freed from an overbearing concern to achieve perfection with each individual stroke. We are not even required to consider chasing our mistakes. Consequently, we can swing free. As we make each solid shot, we need to take the time to internalize the result. By becoming a diligent witness to successful outcomes, as we learn to dismiss failure, we begin a process of reconditioning the subconscious mind. If we continue to bombard our subconscious self with positive results we have no option but to accept our fullest potential as the norm. Then we gain the ability to control the input to the subconscious mind. We are now able to open ourselves to the powerful thinking of possibilities, taking our thoughts away from the absolute fear that lies within negative, thinking patterns.

The game of golf, by its nature, is very imposing on our thought process. When we ready ourselves for each stroke, opening the floodgates to what can go wrong, we have not anchored enough accepted instances of positive outcome into our subconscious. The mind-set is therefore conditioned in a defensive posture, leading to reluctant indecisiveness. If we focus on the intensions of the moment we risk opening our mind to accept conditioning from negative responses. This type of neurological programming has a devastating impact on our attitude and creates a destructive momentum. Taking on a commitment to put in the necessary rehearsal time pays off many times over, as our brain becomes conditioned to accept our capabilities to achieve a free-flowing play. When we develop the ability to align within a commitment and fully connect to the process of development, our pleasurable experiences are restored. This allows us to overcome the resistance of subconscious interference.

Indecisive Acceptance

There are times on the course when we are lured into a state of complacency. It could come from a physical, mental, or spiritual inadequacy that has a very destructive impact on our fundamental passion. This produces a sequential, controlling effect that invades our attitude and renders the purpose meaningless. These are the moments when our subconscious allows phrases such as *it doesn't really matter anyway, who cares, or what difference does it make* to seep into our thoughts. This frame of mind points us down a path of indecisive acceptance of outcome, which diminishes our desire, determination, motivation, and intention toward accomplishment. This path often leads us to a level of apathy and despair. We have within us the human power of choice. A decision can be made on what type of journey we would like to travel, thus avoiding the *oh, whatever* syndrome that seems to be infiltrating our society today, leaving us with a feeling of degeneration and hopelessness.

Each new day opens a momentous opportunity for us to experience our life and quality of the game we choose to play. We consciously decide, first and foremost, not to be uncertain. There is no excuse for indecision if the desire is to help us reach our highest expectations. As we raise ourselves to this level of inner awareness, we educate our minds to stay fully engaged in the process of growth and accomplishment. This awareness allows us to move the spirit of our game play and achieve an enlightened understanding of the purpose of each stroke in life. Our process is now established with a clarity of force that dismisses the negative impulses lying dormant within the mental gremlins of the mind.

Many times, we accept indecision because we are put into a situation that provides many options for choice. This has an effect of producing its own anxiety that intrudes on our sensibility and produces the possibility of a painful outcome. Now, our defense mechanisms kick in, allowing for a response to avoid the pain of the wrong decision and instead we simply chose the path of least resistance. An apathetic attitude overtakes our consciousness and results in poorly constructed strokes. Once again, we have succumbed to indecision. Our response is often words like "it's not that important" or "oh, well, better luck next time." These are nothing more than negative, responsive thoughts that attempt to justify our indecisive position. What were we thinking? In truth we were trying to avoid thinking, relieving us from taking decisive action.

If we continue to subconsciously avoid decision making, we have little chance for personal growth or the rewards of higher levels of consciousness. We can never become fully self-realized if we continuously avoid decisions in order to escape the painful result of a wrong decision. Anticipatory regret continues to plague our indecisive nature. Eventually, this will bring us to the ultimate pain of never realizing our full potential.

Perhaps we now can come to an understanding that being indecisive never provides us with the ability to resolve the conflicting choices in our lives. If we are able to train our mind-set to easily accept the responsibility of defined choice then, with conviction of the selection and trust within the faith of our spirit, we can open to the divine guidance of the law of attraction. We have to remember that if we remain open to life's experiences, there are truly no wrong choices or decisions. Every option we select opens us to a new level of growth and gracious acceptance of the course within our life's game.

Learning Personality

In order for us to truly become students of our game, we must become fully involved in a clearly defined process that opens a deliberate, comprehensive path. For us to achieve at this level, we need to first become aware of our individual learning behavior and then channel it toward the task we are attempting to master. As we become more actively involved with the integration of our two hemispheres and how they function, we realize the necessity of being connected to our individual dominance. If we are right brain dominant, we need to develop holistic methods of taking in the necessary knowledge. Left brain dominance aligns with a more step-by-step method of acquiring information moving from the parts to the whole in a linear progression.

Through my teaching experience, I have found that left brained students prefer to have the methodology of a swing technique broken down into component parts and then systematically assembled into a whole. However, my right brain dominant students prefer being introduced to the entire swing first. They learn the kinesthetic feel of a swing and then easily break the process into the component parts. Now they can refine the smaller motor skills necessary for their continued development as they maintain a connection to the whole.

If you feel better suited in a systematic approach or a sequential path of learning you are probably left brain oriented. On the other hand, if your right brain is in control of processing information, then your attitude would be one of a *show me how* method to become acquainted with new techniques. As you continue in your development, look for the indicators of dominance and you will be able to progress along a path of least resistance.

Once we have gained enough experience in realizing our learning process, the command of a preference of right or left brained input then begins to connect the opposite hemisphere in a communicative effort, achieving more acceptable playability. Our process of learning carries over to the pursuit of playing. This allows a full connection to a comprehensive analysis for decision making, while maintaining an intuitive feel in the execution of intent.

The process continues to evolve as we maintain a patient attitude to internalize experiences to the point where thoughtful play becomes second nature. At first, we become easily frustrated with our incompetence. At this stage, we do not have the necessary experience to be completely cognizant of why we were able to accomplish our intended stroke and achieve the desired result. Even though we have a vague comprehension of technical know-how, we have not had enough internalization of positive results to support those decisions. We must have faith as we continue to practice and play. We eventually arrive at a point of full acceptance of our potential. Consequently, this next door opens our desire to comprehend at a higher level. We begin to ask meaningful questions and put the answers into learning and playing procedures. Eventually, we begin to know that the attempts remain outside of our comfort zone.

Rehearsal is a must in a routine of regular effort. Although practice has its challenges, the process still remains stimulating as you begin to sense your potential. You have ultimately arrived at the final stage. Comprehensive understanding and command of the golf swing has been realized. Your thought process rejects the possibility of a negative outcome. This process holds true in every aspect of your game. A wholly connected, placid harmony with techniques, tools, and thinking behavior aligns with your purpose. You are now on the way to becoming a true student of the game, fully engaged with and connected to your learning personality.

If desire and intent remain in position of determined effort and honest commitment, a distant view of the next plateau of higher ground remains in our sight.

Chapter Fourteen

Setting Your Sights

Priorities of Play

As we continue our inquiry into the unique nature of golf, our experiences with its complexities stimulates a desire to develop a process of discovery. For many players, simply getting the ball airborne seems to be the only motivation for their effort. This task becomes their main concern. Lying just beneath that intent is the fundamental reason why the ball seems to be so earthbound. Their priority must first shift away from the desire to lift the ball off the turf by using an upward motion of the hands and arms. This desire is a subconscious tendency that plays on our instinctive response in a determined effort to achieve the results.

We realize the process is effortlessly achieved when the ball lies in the pathway of a well executed swing. In the pursuit of our goals, we need to specifically comprehend where the emphasis must be placed. Should our goal be to lift the ball off the ground or to learn the aspects of a proper swing that allows it to become airborne? Simply said, is it better to create a process or procedure as the goal, rather than to forcing a desired result?

Part of the captivating nature that the spirit of the game offers is in the specific requirements of play where the environment is highly defined. The nature of the concept of par as an artificial standard of accomplishment imposes on our priorities and distorts our perceptions.

Rather than accepting a current state of ability, we tend to go out and try to achieve the impossible. Standing on the tee, as an example, our mind tends to shift from the fundamental understanding of the need to execute a stable swing, to a controlling mentality in an attempt to hit the ball as perfectly as possible. The challenge of traversing the distance from tee to green has a daunting visual attraction. The perception has the power to cause a reactive response which alters our primary intent. The goal shifts to acquiring distance and accuracy, instead of the commitment to the fundamentals of the swing. This usually causes the application of additional force resulting in a dislocation in position. The arms and hands are now ahead of our body resulting in a shot that is pulled to the left, snap hooked, or a combination of both. Awareness of what the goal should be is what eventually produces the consistency that we are attempting to achieve. It is necessary for us to convince our mind to be clear about the purpose of the goals. Our thoughts should always be directed toward a fundamental objective that focuses on process not achievement of results. This concept cannot be over emphasized.

Regardless of what type of shot we are playing, from a full swing down to the twelve inch putt, our mind must be focused on the process, with proper intent that fully accepts the potential of positive outcome. As we learn to establish our goals within this thought pattern, our expectations are realized in a calmness of acceptance that reduces the anxiety of the moment. It is better to say to ourselves, "Execute the method in the technique with ease and grace," than "don't make a foolish error of judgment." We must establish a mind-set oriented towards a precise focus on the cause and effect relationship of execution. During times of rehearsal on the practice tee, we should attempt to instill this attitudinal adjustment with each stroke played, instead of aimlessly striking one ball after another. An acceptable, disciplined intention of thoughts can result in a well-designed game plan.

Finally, we should be aware of the level of achievability of the anticipated result. Expectations should be just outside of our capability and experience, but not so far out that the play would be made on a wing and a prayer. This type of structured attitude always provides challenge for growth without causing inhibition. Now, as you review your acquired skills at the current levels of accomplishment, you can begin to establish criteria for your priorities moving forward. The following series of questions helps establish a plan of action.

- **What skills do I need to work on?**
- **What information or knowledge would be helpful?**
- **What assistance do I need and from whom?**
- **What resources do I need?**
- **What could block my progress?**
- **What assumptions am I making?**
- **What ways could I do things better?**
- **What are my limiting beliefs?**

Whatever answers you have to these questions, you must always continue to set your course and pursue your process with passionate determination.

Beginning Now

Regardless of how long we have been involved in playing the game, we should always remain open to the possibilities that lie just outside of our reach. Settling for a position in life easily leads to a monotonous existence of apathy and complacency, which is not supportive of a passionate existence. To achieve a supercharged life force, we should strive for a growth experience that motivates action. As we begin to accept and come into alignment with our ability and expectation, the longing for the next frontier of the journey pulls us in a direction of visionary expansion and recharges our desire. Being fully immersed in the experience of living provides the exhilaration of passionate involvement. We cannot just wait for the next experience on our course of choice, but rather we must seize the opportunity and *go fore it*.

If we are to remain true to our intentions and desires, we must continue the efforts as if we are starting on the next leg of the excursion. We have no knowledge of the joy that may come our way or the hardships that we will need to overcome, but if we maintain an absolute faith in an ability to proceed, we are given the powerful strength of conviction through our connection to the game. Lives continue to unfold in the manner determined by intended purpose, manifested through the evolution of a process. We once again become the architects of our course design. As we proceed along the way, self-confidence expands and awareness of possibilities creates a vision of our new reality. Self-motivation is not imposed, but becomes automatic. There is no stopping us. That is what winning is truly about and is not defined by the posted score. Winning or losing is only recognized by the structure of the process, supported by a cornerstone, filled with strong personal values and concerns.

We need to continue our assessment and evaluate where we currently are (the reality), where we would like to be (a visionary destiny), and how we are going to get there (the game plan). In addition, we need to select our support team. Who are the people that we count on to be positively connected with the vision? We must also be careful about our acceptance of negative input from poisonous comments from the people that surround us. Although not deliberately malicious on their part, others can sometimes impart a strong effect on our beliefs. We must, therefore, not hold back in expressing our intent to those who show even the slightest amount of interest. When we re-affirm intentions by making positive statements about what we wish to accomplish, we are able to accept them as our destiny and believe in their absolute achievability.

As our growth and achievement continue to expand, it is important to have an ongoing process of assessment and evaluation. Keeping a daily journal is helpful and also extremely therapeutic. Hold nothing back, let the words flow and just write. Evaluate the content later, after you record your free-flowing thoughts. Efforts need to be supported by the clarity of our concepts. Self-confidence is easily increased or decreased based on the quality of our ideas. If the thinking process takes us down a road of easy acceptance of our current state of being, we lose self-confidence and become uninspired. We should continue to challenge the development of a current state of playability in all that we do. As we continue to be aware, care is taken to not be so obsessed with growth that we exert too much pressure on ourselves and lose sight of the purpose. Our striving should always support a sense of thriving with the enjoyment that rejuvenates the spirit with the recognition of achievement.

Overcoming Obstacles

Consciously setting our mind's desire on purposeful achievement is a worthwhile pursuit that has a positive impact on our feelings of self-worth and confidence. Along with this mind-set comes a responsibility to position and accept a well-formed course of action that must be met without resistance. The self-discipline to carry out the elements of the decisive action plan must be unfailing if we are to become self-actualized in our accomplishment. When all is going well, this game plan seems to be reasonable, if not inspirationally motivating. But what happens when we hit any type of resistance in the process, experience some type of setback, or stagnation? When the spirit is infiltrated with the painful feeling of loss of control in our ability to overcome any interference, then many times a defense mechanism kicks in. An unconscious avoidance of challenges blocks the directional path and imposes itself on our will. We experience a fight or flight syndrome that becomes a test of one's true courage.

When we consciously decide to better ourselves, we have a tremendous opportunity to strengthen the development of our character. This care and nurturing is certainly a worthwhile pursuit that positions us for the accomplishment of whatever we desire. It is the core values that lie within this strength of character that overcomes the obstacles that interfere with passionate purpose. If we can maintain patience, our perseverance is intensified. We are able to accomplish anything that we perceive to be worthwhile. No obstacle stands in our way. The vision becomes our reality as we journey through a course of playful existence.

The game of golf offers us a challenge of pursuit that serves as an example for us to live by. If we are willing to open ourselves to the wonders of the game within the pristine, tranquil environment in which it is played, we can achieve the magical experience of a well-timed, rhythmic sensation in our play. We produce ball contact and propelled flight that escapes its earthbound position and flies with precision to its pre-determined destination. Now, we begin to realize the capability that lies inside each of us to achieve our heart's desire and overcome the obstacles that lie in our path. There is no water hazard too large, no sand bunker that deep, and no undulating green so severe that deters us from our pursuit.

As human beings traveling on a celestial path of divine guidance, we need to accept the responsibility for our continued growth as well as the expansion of all our desired accomplishments. What we need to do is make the commitment, gain the necessary knowledge, acquire the tools of the trade, and joyously pursue our game plan. A path to self-realization is always presented with challenges. The ability to persevere with a determined effort records our final achievement. The number on the scorecard will be the *result of* and *not the purpose for* the accomplishment of our goals. With this mind-set, we can overcome any obstacles along the way.

Moving On

As we move through the journey of life, we are presented with a multitude of experiences leading us on in what seems to be a predetermined course of choice. We continue to make plans, set our sights, establish goals, and attempt to control our destiny, only to find out that we have arrived at a momentary resting place. Looking back, in hindsight, we realize that every decision was made dependent upon its own set of consequences that required a new plan of action. In the game of golf, this is an ongoing necessity, which, if embraced, has the power to raise our consciousness to heightened levels of awareness. Every stroke we make on the course is directed toward a very specific goal, however, due to the imperfection of our fundamental humanness, we can easily deviate from the original intention. We are presented with a whole new set of circumstances to consider as we determine the next plan of action. Our trek around the course becomes anything but a straight line. The mental expectation of the multiple changes in direction that are necessary provides the opportunity to encounter the experiences stimulating our creative character. This is why we are both intrigued and humbled by this particular sport. *It* is what keeps us coming back.

We must have a sense of direction, a road map that provides a plan of travel to reach our ultimate destination. As we continue on the journey, we are confronted by the decisive action plan that directs our travel. There is so much that we anticipate along the way. It is the unexpected that challenges our determination and tenacity and stirs the faith we have in the ability to creatively deal with the various alterations on our adventure. When we are open to the possibility of detour within the game plan, then we are able to travel a chosen path with a sense of graceful assuredness that instills within our character a state of steadfast intent, desire, and unyielding determination. This also transfers and holds true in our lives off the golf course.

As self-actualized players of the game, we develop the sense of quiet confidence that provides the openness so necessary to accept the messages channeled through our spiritual guidance system. This provides us with the necessary strength of conviction in our decisive action which easily accepts the interruptions to our carefully designed, goal-oriented game plan. As we near our destination, we look back on our experience and most vividly remember the excitement of the challenges presented. We become most inspired and reassured by our ability to accept the challenge of a misdirected decision and rectify it through our creative, instinctive sensibility. We are now filled with an exhilaration that only comes from an initial challenge that has been overcome by our own individual efforts. We have arrived, better for our experience, and on a higher plane of human existence than before we left. After a period of restful rejuvenation, we open ourselves to the contemplation of our next course of action. We formulate new goals from a higher plane of existence. The next challenge presents itself at the right time and in the right way. We must stay open to the possibilities and feel a sense of confidence in a commitment to play. The next round in the quest for achieving the experimental growth in our process presents additional opportunities. As the journey continues to unfold, we allow ourselves to move on undeterred in a commitment for expansion.

Higher Ground

Each new day brings exciting new opportunities to try to uncover potential directional forces. The spiritual acceptance of the universal cosmic connection provides us with an open-minded view of the unfolding, developmental process. Our abilities are challenged by the unexpected circumstances as we encounter them. These become a motivation to overcome the next level of endurance, calling on aspects of our consciousness and patience that move the processing potential to a higher ground of existence. Passion for living with open awareness and continuous clarity of purpose is instilled in the creation of a playful process leading us toward our achievable pursuit. The continuum passing from passion to purpose to process to pursuit continues to expand our human character and moves us to higher ground. This allows for more solid contact with each new stroke on this newly found course of existence.

As we continue onward, we should always be open and ready to play the next round of golf, one stroke at a time, leading to a final score that supports our purpose. We must, however, realize that the score may not just add up and support the expectation or resemble our true capabilities. It is in how the round is played that sets the course of a player's existence. Each of us has within our nature a game of higher achievability waiting to be inspired by the small, incremental moments of expansion toward our ultimate potential. If desire and intent remain in position of determined effort and honest commitment, a distant view of the next plateau of higher ground remains in our sight.

Encountering the new experience of each round of golf brings a certain amount of anxiety and anticipation presented by the challenge of the higher ground. At times, our resistance to the possibilities of the challenges that our travels present seem more than we can accept. Fear of failing and encountering a setback in our perception of self-worth can, at times, have a devastating effect. We must remember that our character as human beings was not built on a series of successes, but it was continually strengthened by determination to overcome disappointments and defeats. How we face up to the challenge becomes a more critical component to the ongoing pursuit than any level of success or failure. Therefore, there is no challenge to our game too great or infinitely small that does not have the power to alter the value of our character. As we attempt each stroke, the opportunity presented by the challenge is channeled away from the anticipation of the outcome. This is instilled within the realization of each body movement which opens to the spiritual acceptance of human possibilities. The result of an achievement allows for the next building block of acceptable belief structure in the development of our golfing lives.

Upon arriving on the higher ground of a newly discovered course, we encounter the fairways and greens of our future play that stimulate conscious awareness. We once again subject ourselves to the innocent vulnerability that is dependent upon the achievement of our result. As we move from hole to hole, we must stay in focus with the moment and accept the consequences of play. Our *response ability* remains in a state of total involvement with clear intent. We expect the experience to be fully supportive of the established process as we commit to a fully engaged game. We will always remember what a remarkable game *it* is that we have the privilege to play. Our priorities must remain within proper perspective as we continue setting our sights on the higher ground of continued expansion.

If we are helped to conceive a process that offers possibility, then we will achieve and receive the attitude, aptitude, and altitude that we desire. A belief in ourselves supports the rise over run that produces the desired trajectory in the best stroke of our lives.

Chapter Fifteen

Maximizing Potential

Moment of Inertia

Sir Isaac Newton surmised that objects in motion tend to stay in motion with the same speed and the same direction unless acted upon by an outside force. Newton further stated that objects at rest tend to stay at rest unless acted upon by an outside force. The game of golf clearly demonstrates this natural law. Through the process of our playing a golf shot, we approach the position of our ball lying dormant on the turf waiting to be sent airborne. However, the ball is not sent into infinite flight in the straight intended line of our desire. It must come to rest because of outside forces such as air density, direction of flight, or the gravitational pull of the earth. The ball does not necessarily head in the same direction as predicted or desired due to the result of a less than perfect swing. The final outcome will not necessarily result in the original intent of the player involved since variables are always present.

Just as the natural laws exist, but do not guarantee perfection of outcome, we too become a variable within the multiple aspects of our ball striking ability. Our psychological, physiological, spiritual, and yes, even our sociological makeup on any given day will add their own element of deviation from a straight line of flight. From the wholeness of our being, we need to seek the balance necessary to create a state of acceptance that positively affects the moment of inertia. There are days when we wake up in the morning and just do not want to put in the effort. Tasks of the day either seem too overwhelming or mundane. The affect that these states of consciousness have on our well-being are quite profound. Sometimes they have the power to paralyze us or leave us with a sense of overwhelming desperation. It is at these moments that we find hidden opportunity to expand our core character and rise above the circumstances of the time and place. This is what builds the strength of a cornerstone of willpower. Many of us, from time to time, would just as soon pull the covers over our head ducking and hiding from responsibility. We become the victims of self-imposed moments of inertia, simply giving in to the demands of our situation while surrendering to disappointment and despair. The direction that our inertia is taking us must be acted upon by an outside force in order to alter the outcome. As human beings we are blessed with the capacity to make choices and the willpower to decide the path of direction that changes our course of action. *It* is simply a question of mind over matter, but if we do not exercise mindfulness, *it* may not matter.

Similar situations occur from shot to shot on the course, as well as in life. At times, we become so elated by the way things are going, that we get caught up in a moment of inertia devoid of fear, pain, and self-doubt. Our passion is soaring and the purpose is clearly defined. The process is so well established within a kinesthetic acceptance of our ability that the pursuit of intensions is locked into the flow zone of a process. We are now moving in effortless forward motion. Then, all of a sudden and seemingly out of nowhere, disaster strikes. An outside force breaks the momentum of our forward movement. The force might be an overconfident disbelief in what we are attempting to accomplish or perhaps not paying careful attention to the swing process. All we know is that our momentum has been altered and is headed off course and out of bounds. The action we take from here and what choices we make determine our eventual outcome. We must be able to dig deep into the spiritual essence of our true purpose. There, we find the directional guidance that overcomes the inertia of potential disaster. As we return to the reliability of our process, we discover the pathway to maximizing the power of inertia at any given moment in our lives.

Rise over Run

As individuals, each of us wants to aspire to our highest capability. With growth and achievement comes the good feeling of accomplishment, which sparks our enthusiasm and brings us to new and exciting levels of spirit filled joy for life and living. We have all experienced those moments when we are totally energized by some happening that was beyond our greatest expectation. Or, perhaps a challenge presents itself that seems greater than what we feel we can deal with. However, somehow, from somewhere, we rise to the occasion, and become resourceful enough to overcome our circumstances. In these moments, our wholeness of mind, body, and spirit congruently accepts the harmonious sense of our well-being. We have an opportunity to store this sense of rightness and connection to the energy that lies within us. The inspiration comes from outside of the controls we would like to impose on our conditional existence. We are presented with the moment of choice that draws on the power within our self-determination as we exercise our right to direct our own destiny. Once again, we are provided with an opportunity to move beyond the limiting beliefs and expand conscious acceptance of full potential to maximize our life experience.

In order to become students of the game, our efforts and commitment must be directed, focused, and fully involved. Each round of golf is sure to unfold in a new and unexpected form that will present heartwarming joy and heartbreaking sorrow. As we allow ourselves to be fully engrossed in all of its requirements, we are freed to completely engage in exercising the highest levels of our self-determination. Now we are relieved from external influence of the opinions, attitudes, and judgments of others and achieve a higher realization of our own self-worth. When we make a choice of total commitment, our self-determination takes hold and we are no longer affected by influences outside of ourselves that might cause a mental, physical, emotional, or spiritual breakdown. We can avoid being robbed of the energy source so necessary for our endurance.

There are times in life and the game that we feel a sense of exhaustion. We may have run out of energy, enthusiasm, time, money, ideas, desires, or intent. How can we begin to overcome these moments and regain the sense of great exhilaration? This is when it becomes extremely important to understand the necessity for balance in our pursuit of maximum potential. Periodically, we must allow ourselves the proper amounts of time for refueling and recovery in order to rebuild the strength to encounter the next round of our golf or life experience. With newly found rejuvenation, we can once again move forward as we call upon our past encounters to inspire and motivate our determination and self-empowerment.

We become aware that the challenge of rising to higher levels of potential is certainly a chosen path worth taking. It requires the utmost awareness of proper care and consideration. In achieving at a satisfying level of support for our true self-worth, we must immerse ourselves in a supportive environment of inspiration and knowledge. It is crucial to seek the type of instructional coaching that brings out our best efforts without imposing overbearing and/or unachievable mandates. If we are helped to conceive a process that offers possibility, then we will achieve and receive the attitude, aptitude, and altitude that we desire. A belief in ourselves supports the rise over run that produces the desired trajectory in the best stroke of our lives.

Attitude, Aptitude, and Altitude

If we are to expand ourselves to levels of existence that allow us to thrive within the splendor of our life's experience, we need to become absolutely committed to a total involvement in a day-to-day effort. Maintaining the stamina to overcome challenges of our willful desire and determination allows us to make choices that bring us to a sense of attitudinal well-being. If we stay in a positive state of mind, our capacity for expansion remains open and receptive. This, in turn, allows an intellectual development to receive information and store knowledge, which can be retrieved in any future encounters. The opportunity is present to expand our aptitude as we acquire these new and challenging experiences. Expecting the exhilaration in a sense of consistent renewal of passion for life, we playfully pursue the necessities of our existence. We can create a realized acceptance of a positive relationship to even the most demanding or routine requirements.

We are now on a path of grateful existence and acceptance leading to an enlightened elevation of an ability that transcends the daily grind and adds new meaning to our work and play. I have consistently found that the attitudes that I consciously maintain provide strength of commitment, both on and off the golf course. What I have come to realize is that by remaining positive in our outlook through constructive, creative thinking, we are able to consistently elicit an optimistic anticipation of future encounters. Expecting a successful outcome as we play each round instills a belief in our ability to remain motivated to carry out the goals that have been set. We are able to face the disappointment of our errant shots as blessed opportunities, even during the times of despair. Solutions can be explored to the problems that provide us with new, higher levels of comprehension. Now, we become better equipped and more inspired to *go fore it* on our journey to higher ground. Even the most demanding or routine requirements of what needs to be accomplished will never overwhelm us.

By not giving up or giving in we are choosing a path of happiness paved with increasing confidence and belief. As self-realized and self-determined students of our game, we begin to encounter opportunities for our betterment in every situation and circumstance. As we stroll down fairways filled with gleaming sunlight, we can manifest constructive changes in our golf game which will inspire all aspects of our lives. We continue to build our game around this illuminated outlook, attracting players within our sphere of influence to encourage, who go on to motivate others. Our golfing environments are lifted to another plane of existence. We have been given a gift from the Golf Gods to become dedicated as purposeful players of the game. To inspire others is a blessing from the core of our divine, spiritual connection. When the golf spirit is soaring at this level, our love for the game becomes contagious.

The game of golf can truly live inside of us as a guiding force in our life with the power to create, support, and expand the development of a positive and determined character. Our involvement in the game continues to grow in an unhurried acquisition of experience, knowledge and aptitude for accomplishment becomes progressively more open to all possibilities. Attitudes are supported and beliefs in capacity for achievement are accepted and realized. We are now prepared to begin the next leap forward to new heights of experience as the process continues to present a course that guides the pursuit and maximizes our potential.

Quantum Leaps

Many times in our efforts to maximize potential we have a tendency to have such a high level of determination that we become our own resistance barrier. This easily happens as we pursue the various aspects, methodologies, techniques, and fundamentals in our golfing pursuits. There is a necessary digestion of information before we can expect an experience to catch up with our knowledge. Consequently, each time we arrive at a new level of playability, we can expect to plateau before the next growth spurt occurs. By remaining vigilant in our awareness of this, we can still remain balanced between patience and growth. This is why it becomes so important to understand the concept of the necessity for growth. Any pursuit in life requires properly timed input of knowledge, practice, and play through the acquisition of instruction. We should allow adequate time to internalize the new information without an unrealistic expectation of miraculous, instant change in ability level.

If the commitment remains focused, we avoid possible complacency, which could occur if we settled for results not matching our capabilities. It is important to keep the goals for achievement clear, while remembering to enjoy the pursuit. When we are consistent with our commitment for improvement, the rewards miraculously appear, delivering the instantaneous result for which we strive. Now, the life force of the game is rapidly revealed and moves effortlessly into our grasp. We unexpectedly achieve a quantum leap, but we must first be willing to fully trust this leap of faith. Trust comes from experience and increased knowledge. Blind faith that has no substance must rely on experience and vision. We have all said at one time or another "when all else fails or here goes nothing," not always realizing the sense of hopelessness or despair we seem to have developed. Instead, we have to continue the playful pursuit in a carefully designed process that provides the continued evolution of our capability. Within this process we can often quickly find solutions to the problems we encounter. The flashes of intuitive understanding and capability arrive progressively faster and more often. A new momentum is established and fueled by renewed resourceful energy. We should not be surprised to experience a series of positive outcomes during this period of good fortune. At these times we are in total alignment with a spiritual strength of conviction that taps the divine guidance that exists within the passion for our activity. On the golf course we are improving our score with no forceful intent. It is just happening in the most natural way. We are now at a moment of quantum transition in attitude, posture, and belief, which lifts self-confidence to a state of total acceptance of the possibilities that lie before us.

Our game play is now cooperating with intent and effort. We gain deeper understanding of the process as we are doing non-doing produced by a trusting subconscious acceptance of belief in our capabilities. The game can now open to opportunities that we may not have considered before exposing the potential for the next quantum leap. Movement forward is harmonious with our being in complete acceptance and grateful awareness. We embrace the insightful understanding of our process of self-realized creation, which results in a calm inner sense of well-being. Growing wiser in our nature we have come ever closer to the unfolding of a cosmic connection.

Infinite Wisdom

Golf provides an experience throughout a lifetime that inspires and expands a self-realization, allowing for a profound contemplation of purpose. Within all of us, there is a place of retreat that is quiet and serene where we can go to understand what goes well beyond conventional thinking. This inner dwelling bypasses the intellectual capabilities of our rational thought processes. It somehow seems to evoke a much more logical conclusion than any methodical approach could ever produce. As we continue our pursuit of the intricacies of the game, we begin to witness varying moments of unexplained greatness. Guided by an intuitive sensibility of reacting correctly, we often try to impose action without involving conscious thought processes. We are captivated by an effortless power that came from our highest levels of passionate play. This enables us to gain the insight that allows for our participation in golfing and living that can open awareness to the splendor of all existence. This is truly the moment that we begin to realize a connection to the universal spirit that runs through all that is.

We need to understand that our awareness has come to us from the universe of divine knowledge of infinite existence, sometimes referred to as from the "no where" to the present moment of "now here." The sense of rightness within our momentary choices is instantaneously recalled. Sensible decisions are provided at the exact moment of need, producing perfection in our desired result with no preconditioned effort. Having this gift of infinite wisdom within us we transcend all that we know. Golf requires this powerful human aspect if we are to reach our full potential.

We are able to overcome the resistant barriers and limitations that ground our possible, expanded capability. As our potential energy is released, we overcome a resting inertia and activate a kinetic exhilaration of realized accomplishment. Poised and ready to allow our inner power of this endless wisdom, we express its full impact on an extraordinary capability. Willful desire is delivered to us from parts unknown. Participation is now witnessed in our play through a whirlwind of exhilaration that reverberates within us. We are in tune with the music of the spheres. The creative impulses that spring forth in the divine moments of this level of cosmic connection can easily be denied by our rational left brained gremlins, as they attempt to squelch inspiration. Inspired moments of achievement are over analyzed and thereby restrict the content of true character, accepting the wisdom that opens us to our infinite potential. Guarding against this interference we must question last minute thoughts as we play each stroke of our game. Instinct moves us to the realizations of possibilities that exist just outside of our current comfort zones that begin to achieve beyond our greatest expectations. As we release our inhibitions and reach for new levels of courage and conviction we begin to follow a path of an enlightened golfing adventure. This serves as an example of how to pursue any endeavor that is worthwhile. We learn to trust our infinite wisdom on our journey to realize our maximum potential.

Part Four

The Pursuit

As we travel on the many paths that life offers, we encounter a multitude of possible experiences from which to choose. Each choice opens to us a world of discovery that lies within our grasp and awaits a passionate involvement. Strength of commitment and level of interest determines our willingness to become involved in the study of the activity. If a connection to the purpose is realized, a marvelous possibility for continued growth develops. The process of living, working, and playing becomes enhanced by a passionate pursuit of a newly discovered opportunity that stimulates our imagination.

In order to achieve this type of experience in the game of golf, we must allow ourselves the privilege of becoming students of the game. Today, information is readily available to the player, but inspiration must be sought from many sources. We must cautiously filter the information to which we are exposed. The careful attention of a highly qualified golf instructor is crucial. Your coach should assist you in your pursuit while becoming a trusted friend and confidant. You should, however, put in the necessary work of regularly scheduled practice, rehearsal, and play. This becomes a very stimulating part of your routine that lifts you out of the doldrums and restores your vitality.

Having a passionate commitment in pursuing an activity that is outside of your normal routine adds a new dimension to your life. Golf, unlike any other sport, is surrounded by tradition, dignity, and integrity that present a standard of excellence by which to live. What better involvement can we look to for inspiration and motivation? The days on the course create an opportunity to encounter a total sense of well-being. In an environment of peaceful harmony an inner connection to the game unfolds. Passionate commitment to physical fitness, mental acuity, and psychological stability supports an understanding of our basic humanity. The purpose continues to fulfill a process for our continued pursuit.

I feel assured that I will continue my own pursuit to be the best that I can be as both a teacher and student of the game. My efforts are focused on generating a passion that defines a clarity of purpose. Future days will be spent sharing my lifelong commitment to this game. Golf has been a motivational guidepost to my direction in life. As my students open up to a spiritual centering through their heartfelt pursuit, they begin to understand what *it* is that the game represents and what I discovered along the way.

Purpose now shifts away from an intention for controlling outcome to one of allowing the process to be revealed. A metamorphosis unfolds, moving the student from a participant in the game of golf to becoming a student of the game.

Chapter Sixteen

Student of Your Game

The Golfer Within

When we are open to a new experience in life, it is a wise idea to align with a mentor who will guide our journey and help us on a path to a successful outcome. After the many years spent as a teaching professional I have come to realize the importance of a proper introduction to the game. I feel blessed to have had the privilege of getting to know my students on many levels. As I learn more about who they are and what they want to achieve, I am able to come up with the proper prescription to help them overcome their insecurities, fears, anxiety, and limiting beliefs. It is a wonderful experience to witness the blossoming of the golfer that I believe resides in all of us, just waiting for the chance to express the childlike enthusiasm of a newly found accomplishment in life. As my students and I join in the pursuit, we begin to come together and develop a wonderful sense of cooperative effort. My goal is to achieve more than the teaching of the techniques, fundamentals, and procedures. The students I serve are invited on an inquiry into the heart and soul of the passionate involvement that I share in my transfer of knowledge. Hopefully each of them walk away, lifted and inspired to become diligent and involved in the pursuit of one of life's most worthwhile endeavors.

The game of golf is a relatively easy game to learn. I know that this goes very much against popular belief, but after more than thirty years of teaching, I have witnessed countless numbers of students achieving at a reasonable capability. As they experience a very satisfying, recreational relationship to the game their enthusiasm is enhanced. In return I receive such joy in watching a beginner's rejuvenated, childlike wonder exploding as they make their first solid contact with the ball. Their natural sense of body flow brings a level of connectedness in their restorative faith and trust. From that point on, they move past the fear of failure and are opened to an honest experience in their freedom of play. This is all made possible due to the "perfection of connection" of the various parts of the human body. I am convinced that God designed our bodies to play golf. When the golf swing is generated from the turn of the shoulders, rather than with only the arms and hands, the rest of the body falls naturally into position. The arms, hands, hips, knees, and feet do exactly what they are supposed to do. Our weight shifts from left to right (for right-handed players and opposite for left-handed players) on the back swing and right to left on the downswing and follow through. The ball simply gets in the way. If we don't think too much about deliberately trying to hit the ball it has a good chance of coming into a very acceptable contact with the face of our club. We experience a magical moment of perfect contact.

Why then, is it so difficult to be consistent with our ball striking? The answer lies in the feeble capacity that our brain has in understanding that it cannot deliberately control and carry out its methodical intent. So our brain tells us swing hard, instead of allowing a rhythmic flow that permits the ball to be properly struck. We must learn to trust the force that we have discovered which now resides inside of us.

At Winding Hills Golf Course I teach an ongoing series of mental game lessons that provides the student with a significantly improved understanding of how the hemispheric differences affect our ability to comprehend the complex nature of mind over matter. My goal has always been to bring my students into an alignment with the mind, body, and spiritual synergy providing a participation of unhampered pursuit of their game. The peace of mind and tranquility that golf has the power to deliver emerges and supports a determined effort. This is the life force that sustains and provides an enthusiastic learning experience. This reveals the spiritual connection to the golfer who lies within all who attempt to learn and play as they become committed students of the game.

Learning Continuum

When something in our lives commands attention and raises curiosity, we look to a methodology that allows us to pursue the necessary abilities to satisfy this hunger. Passion will only carry us to a certain point, beyond which our growth and development is limited. As a process of creative inquiry and acquisition of knowledge motivates our desire to become more actively involved, we discover or develop a guidance system for learning. Through my own continuing dedication to this game, I have learned a process of self-realized steps in my own behavior that I now use in my work as a golf instructor. I refer to this as the learning continuum. This was briefly introduced earlier in the book, but it is important to understand this method of acquiring knowledge in further detail at this time.

If we are to become proficient, repetition must be an integral part of the process. Mastery can only be achieved after multiple allowances of full integration into the mind, body, and spirit. This process starts with a concept of what *it* is that we are attempting to achieve. First, we must be able to acquire a fundamental methodology to guide us. When applied to the golf swing, we must discover what *it* is and how to make *it* work. This is achieved by witnessing adequate demonstrations coupled with clear, concise verbal explanation. Once we have conceived the *it* of the mechanics, we can begin to experience the process through the trial and error phase of acceptance as we train a kinesthetic *response ability*. Our perception of the how to do *it* is now enhanced and we soon acquire the ability to replicate the behavior. This requires time and effort if concrete understanding is to take place. As we begin to gain a feeling for the correct swing, we move to the perception stage of the continuum.

At this point we are aligned with the mechanics and have had enough experience that the swing becomes more natural in feel, we arrive at the awareness level of perception. We then begin to understand the sensation of the swing and the bodily movement cooperates with our intentions. In short we now can perceive *it*.

Once perceptive abilities are in place, we put the swing into consistent rehearsal on the practice tee. As our acceptance becomes fully engrained, we can achieve a consistency of results that progressively establishes a more powerful belief in the ability to accomplish purposeful intentions. Only then can we accept our potential to achieve *it*. This is the stage where we begin to internalize that we know how and can actually begin to believe *it*.

As our belief system begins to take hold, passion to pursue the game further becomes energized and self-confidence is justified and enhanced. Spiritual connection with the game grows, allowing for a more effortless commitment to the process. Playing takes on a higher purpose of involvement as our self-esteem is strengthened. A new level of momentum is now creating a positive effect on a commitment to the pursuit. If properly realized, golf is a useful parallel to all of life's experiences and can have an effect on the quality of one's strengthening character. We now have established a solid belief system that holds true both in golf and life.

At this point in the quest for self-realization, we are cautious to avoid complacency as our efforts are more easily rewarded. We must be wary of our strongly developing ego since it could have a negative effect as it attempts to infringe on our basic character. If we are not careful, we could easily deceive ourselves and become separated from a dedicated purpose. We can become vulnerable and slip into a deceptive mode of behavior. Each individual accomplishment has set us up to deceive ourselves into believing that we are in full control of our destiny. We may find that we have truly denied the *it factor* of commitment to our game play. This is the moment of awareness and new awakening. Disaster is looming, waiting to strike. We must look deeper inside of ourselves for strong commitment to our basic values and be grateful for the newly perceived, awakened, and enlightened spirit. The ability to choose brings us to only one conclusion, additional rehearsal is necessary. Returning to the practice tee we take decisive action to retrieve the basic concepts that gave us our initial, successful experiences. Our effort to retrieve *it* begins again.

This continuum of learning goes on for as long as our involvement in the pursuit is maintained. Understanding its nature assists tremendously in our acceptance of the human frailties and instills a hopeful continuation of growth and development through our golfing experience and all of life's opportunities. When we can connect our efforts to the pursuit, we become accepting students of golf's life force.

Sensational Strokes

The ability that we have to achieve a properly structured golf swing is dependent on more than just the physical pursuit. When we encounter a situation that requires the highest levels of physical capability, we must be able to elicit other aspects of our human condition. The activation of the psychological acceptance of what is necessary overshadows the physical aspect in the requirements presented. These situations call upon the deepest level of connection to the highest capacity of our golfing capability. Although the challenge may seem to be overwhelming, it is this aspect of our encounter with the uniqueness of the game that provides the highest satisfaction. We have the opportunity to witness the true sense of our ability to execute the stroke. When we are able to carry out the requirements and meet the challenge, the exhilaration of that moment brings us ever closer to the inner spirit of what golf truly offers. We have achieved what we thought was impossible.

As we continue to overcome the adversity by experiencing its existence, confronting its requirement, and accepting our ability to respond to its demands we move to the higher ground of self-realization. A quiet consciousness must be maintained that does not attempt to interfere with the moment of contact. As discussed earlier, the very nature of the game of golf and the highly defined structure of the course, impose a controlling desire to manipulate the flight of the ball. Considerations for distance and direction require precise attention to detail in the execution of each stroke played. It is only by the cooperation between our conscious determination and the subconscious sensibility that we can accept the expansion of our pursuit to the level we are capable of achieving.

As an instructor of the game, it has become part of my desire to awaken my students' subconscious capabilities and allow them an opportunity to connect with a very special part of their mental capacity to play their game. This is an area of their existence that has remained considerably underdeveloped. Most formal education relies primarily on cognitive development that requires the mental storehousing of information to be recalled on demand in order to fulfill the requirement of standardized tests. Unfortunately, our creative instinct cannot fit into the perfectly square hole of definable capability required for accurate scorekeeping. Understanding the fallacy of accountability of outcome creates an artificial standard of excellence, such as par for the course. Passion for participation no longer stimulates life's experiences.

In my teaching process I allow students to learn the fundamentals of the golf swing in a very casual, non-threatening manner, initially relieving them of the desire for perfection. A teaching strategy that I have developed encourages a carefree, experiential involvement which elicits a natural realization and connects the right and left hemispheres of the brain in a cooperative effort. This type of pursuit enables the conscious and subconscious mind-set to become equally involved with the process of accomplishing their goals. From this basic premise comes a transformational aura of natural involvement that overtakes the student with an unlocking of their full potential. They are now ready to experience the joyful sense of awareness in a properly constructed swing. Purpose now shifts away from an intention for controlling outcome to one of allowing the process to be revealed. A metamorphosis unfolds, moving the student from a participant in the game of golf to becoming a student of the game. Their desire is no longer connected to any artificial requirement, but has shifted to a higher plane. This opens their potential, derived from their natural stroke through contact, solidifying their understanding of what *it* is. They have now been liberated to pursue the game in active, uninhibited participation. The level of interest and involvement will continue to grow as their ability is revealed in an effortless flow of enthusiastic play. Lives will be better for the experience as the strokes are released from the depth of each sensation.

Extension and Follow Through

Clarity of intention as a guiding force in the course of life experience and is one of the most important factors that support our ability. It allows us to remain in alignment with the desired result. When we are totally connected to our intent, the ability to overcome any weakness in the spirit provides us with the kinetic energy to persevere. We develop a commitment to complete any task, regardless of its level of significance within the whole of our experience. This attention to detail becomes a natural part of a playful journey rather than a burdensome task. Falling short on the committed actions that support our intent is not an option. Following through on the extension beyond the moment of contact is the guiding force of the pursuit of all of life's opportunities.

Once we achieve acceptance in our capacity for follow through, we are provided with the momentum that allows us to go the distance in our pursuit. This fundamental attitude applied at the right moment within our golf swing is exactly the mind-set needed to provide both the solidity of contact and the required directional ball flight. As we begin to fully apply the purposeful intention of the mechanics of our swing, we train the kinesthetic response into a satisfying sensibility, which becomes a natural part of our free-flowing motion. Effortless accomplishment becomes the consistent reward of our pursuit. If we simply exercise the shift in commitment to what happens after the moment of contact then the rewards will fall into place.

The question still remains, however, how can we elicit the response that allows for this committed effort to be consistently realized? For the answer to this, we must examine the mind-set required to place the process in motion. To accomplish anything in life we must develop a basic guidance system that establishes a standard of unwavering beliefs to which we adhere. These beliefs keep us on the designed course in life. Our purpose becomes staying on the fairway, away from the rough, bunkers, and water hazards that could entrap us with imposing penalties. This is where we can call upon our basic values stabilizing the cornerstone of structural support. If we can remain accountable to our desire for competence and maintain a faith that allows for the freedom that we seek in our game play, we are able to maintain a state of fully accepted commitment and achieve a creative connection that supports the pursuit. Decisiveness in our actions aids in the adventurous discovery that reveals our desire's innovation and opens us for continued personal growth. The pleasure that we derive from the quality of each effort supports the ongoing resourcefulness of our character. Tolerance for disappointment is replaced with a grateful acceptance of human frailty and acts as a springboard for our determined improvement through deliberate execution.

With this comprehensive understanding of a capacity for expansion and follow through, we move one step closer while immersing the experiences that our lives have to offer. Growing in capacity we seize the opportunities that are encountered. We extend follow through within our ongoing pursuit as dedicated students in all of life's opportunities.

Sequential Rhythm

As we begin to accept the natural kinesthetic connections of our body motion, we conceptualize how effortless power is generated through a system of levers and torque that is created by a proper shoulder turn. Even though it is relatively easy to understand, we still have a tendency to attempt to hit the ball more with our arms and hands. Our instinctive nature wants to make the ball take flight rather than allowing it to simply get in the way of a well-timed swing. This causes an improper angle of contact and results in erratic direction and distance. The forceful nature of swinging with our arms and hands becomes the most destructive element of the golf swing. It is within our nature to want to control a muscular strike on the ball. This is misperceived as the intention of our effort. It is essential for us to comprehend the necessity of eliminating the thought from our over-controlling mind and remove feeble attempts of a predetermined outcome.

In order to achieve our ultimate goal of producing effortless power and control, we must study the relationship of rhythm, tempo, timing, and balance, all of which lie at the core of control in the sequential motion of our body. In my years of teaching, I have come to realize that we each have within us a natural body rhythm that moves us through life. I have found that there seems to be a consistency of rhythm that relates to a one second motion. This is experienced if we were to walk at a natural speed and begin to time our steps with a tick tock verbal command applied to the speed of our pace. We would discover a certain comfort of coordinated momentum. Our pace would not be moving excessively fast or too slow and there would be a natural, well-balanced, sensibility of our forward motion. This rhythmic coordination of movement can easily be applied to the rhythm of the golf swing for every stroke, from a full swing with the driver down to the two-inch tap in putt. If we condition our mind to utilize a verbal command as a mantra we begin to gain control of the rhythmic requirement of body motion. Effortless power is achieved when we control the sequential coordination of the leverage produced by the turn of the shoulders, arms, hands, hips, knees, legs, and feet. The study of our body mechanics integrates the structural support in our pursuit of a natural swing.

We must be diligent in our application of the sequential release of the combination of levers, perfectly timed, to create maximum club head speed with an easy and grace of motion. When we are able to stay focused on the process, we begin to come into harmonious congruency of a mind, body, and spirit connection that should always lie at the heart of our fundamental, purposeful pursuit. Through the use of a mantra, we eliminate last minute thoughts that might infringe or disrupt the rhythm and tempo of our perfect balance. Only then are we able to direct the intentions away from our conscious desire to control outcome and are able to tap into a far more powerful aspect of our capacity. This lies within the intuitive sensibility to naturally accept the necessary mechanics of body motion, while achieving a connection to the flow zone of effortless motion. We are finally in touch with the secret of the game. Our playful nature is released as the efforts become a source and motivation for our play. The sequence of happening in golf provides a rhythm that is harmonious with our efforts, intentions, and desires. We are then able to continue our study in balance with the necessities of pursuit while achieving poetry in motion.

Once the club choice is made, then we begin to activate an imaginative capacity in order to pre-condition our sensitivity to the expected outcome. At the start of each hole, the process of imagination begins before the ball is even placed on the tee.

Chapter Seventeen

Rehearsal for Play

Holistic Approach

Any worthwhile endeavor in life offers its own unique opportunity to expand the physical capabilities through our psychological capacities. As we confront the challenges of the activity we must accept a responsibility to become fully engaged in acquiring the necessary skills and knowledge for success. The pursuit of the relative techniques that make up the comprehensive requirements of the activity then evolves in a natural manner. Artificial manipulation of the components of the endeavor must be avoided. The integrity of our fundamental purpose should remain in support of the clarity of intent. As we rehearse the integral parts of our game play, the essential elements join together in a holistic, supportive process of effortless, flowing motion. When we begin to achieve at this higher level of acceptance, we will realize the true purpose. Our ability is revealed in how and where the psychological acceptance of achievement is supported by the cornerstone of beliefs. This strength of character engages in a determination to persevere as we strive to put all of our efforts together into a whole entity. Rehearsing each individual aspect of the game eventually brings us to a point of natural response to whatever is required for any given situation. The ability to break down the intricate necessities of the specific aspects of any activity opens to a fully purposeful pursuit, which accomplishes the end result. Our understanding of the process supports the satisfaction with the outcome of intent. This establishes a comprehensive wholeness in the quality of any experience.

Play, which must be diligently practiced, calls upon the wholeness of our being from all aspects of its methods and techniques. Many times we tend to gravitate toward practicing those things at which we excel. However, we should work equally hard on those aspects that require a more determined repetition in our rehearsal helping us to overcome our weaknesses. Equal time needs to be put into all aspects of our pursuit. We may be able to achieve booming three hundred yard drives, but if we miss too many three foot putts, the totality of achievements can never be completely realized.

There is a direct correlation between each part of the game that reflects on every aspect of the final outcome. In working with different levels of students, I have found that when effort is equally spread across all parts of the game, there is an increased ability to accept disappointment. For example, when a player becomes a reasonably good putter it takes pressure off the necessity for precision in their approach shots. This relaxes the player while easing their stroke and opens them to a higher level of accomplishment. Their ability to produce more consistent pitch and chip shots will, in a similar manner, remove the requirements for more accurate mid and long iron approach shots. The player's full swings allow the necessary freedom of execution that permits a sweet, rhythmic motion, producing solid contact. This same concept continues all the way back to the teeing ground. When the focus of playing each hole is spread over the fundamentals of all aspects of the game, a wholeness of structured process unites and inspires the passionate involvement and strengthens our ability to pursue a more rewarding experience. Through a total commitment to the details of the technical requirements of each individual shot, we are able to unite our capabilities and carry out each aspect of the game's specific demands.

A foundation formed on the understanding of how the various elements combine in harmonious flow offers us a structured study in the pursuit of our gamesmanship. Practice sessions are infused with a deeper sense of purpose, which creates a stronger relativity to our efforts on the course. Playing and rehearsing can now find the proper relativity to support a newfound holistic approach to the complexities of the game.

Pre-shot Routine

When we are committed to a wholeness of our playful pursuit, we are able to meet the demands of a focused execution of every stroke. To be fully connected to the requirement of each specific play, a process of planning is necessary to facilitate the joining of mind, body, and spirit in a oneness of effortless flowing motion. All outside, irrelevant, mental distraction must be eradicated and our minds should become peacefully connected to the clarity of our intentions. In order to accomplish this task, a routine approach to each shot must be created and adhered to with passion. We need to provide for ourselves with a consistent process in order to achieve the confidence that results in reliability. While we properly adopt a pre-shot preparation, we open our sensitivity to the requirements of the moment and tap into an intuitive understanding of precisely what it takes to carry out the intent.

Every player eventually decides on the structure of their own personal routine. However, we need to know the fundamental elements that should always be part of any good procedure. First and foremost, we must check the position of the ball. Depending on the lie, a decision should be made as to what type of shot and club selection would be most advantageous. It is important to realize that distance from the intended target is not always the ultimate consideration. Once the club choice is made, then we begin to activate an imaginative capacity in order to pre-condition our sensitivity to the expected outcome. At the start of each hole, the process of imagination begins before the ball is even placed on the tee. We must look out to our intended target and assess the pros and cons that the design of each hole presents. This determines which side of the tee box would be the most appropriate to hit from. It is imperative that we become willing to trust our sensibility. Once comfortable with our club choice and ball position, we can move onto the physical, mental, and spiritual aspects of the shot.

I often hear my students express concern for ability to aim properly. Consistently I discover that their problem is actually with alignment to the intended target. The idea of aiming has a destructive effect in that it enhances our misguided thoughts of steering the ball to its target. We must trust our set up and alignment, providing for a proper swing path. This process allows the ball to travel on the pre-conceived, intended line of flight established during the pre-shot routine. We are now able to achieve consistent placement of our body position and provide the structural relationship to the ball. Our swing path enables the club face to remain square to the line of flight through impact and produce the maximum force at the moment of contact. Imagining the flight of the ball allows for a pre-conditioned capability to achieve the desired result. This is a key component to the consistency of outcome. If we can foster the habit of lining up our shot from behind the ball, we will be properly positioned to allow a natural acceptance of the projection of the ball flight. To accomplish this, we need to place ourselves in a position that would be the third point in a straight line about six to ten feet behind the ball. Once this is established, we can now visualize the flight of the ball as we move slowly to the set up position. We now begin to place ourselves into alignment, being careful not to set our feet first. Instead, we need to place the clubface square or perpendicular to our perceived line of flight. Our feet can now be properly positioned in relationship to the ball parallel to the target line. It is important to reduce tension by calling on our meditative capabilities to block out all other distractive energies. A deep breath is helpful to allow a settling in the process of acceptance that is required for the careful clearing of our mind. Now we can slip into a state of relaxed certainty that is necessary to become poised and ready for the well structured take away as the backswing begins. Procedures that are consistently established and adhered to in a routine fashion build upon a process of purposeful intent that lies at the cornerstone of the growth and capability in our pursuit. The initial efforts before we swing the club are the determining factor of success or failure. Now, the purpose becomes clear through our pre-shot process as part of our consistent routine of continued pursuit.

Moment of Truth

With proper consideration for the set up complete, we are in correct position for that decisive commitment that we have continually rehearsed. Our minds must now be cleared of thoughts as we slip into the moment of meditative relaxation that supports the congruent, peaceful acceptance of positive outcome. At this point, we have done everything possible to prepare our mind, body, and spirit for the moment of truth. We are now grounded and ready for take away. Staying relaxed and poised at this critical point requires a disciplined, repetitive procedure on the practice tee. Play on the course needs to be connected with the freedom of the practice range where we always had an opportunity to correct our mistakes.

Many of the top players in the world today practice their game by playing the course in their mind's eye. This is not unlike the downhill skier who mentally visualizes their run down the slope. The process allows for a building of confidence that carries a faith of assured commitment to each stroke during competition. As the practice session continues, we are a witness to our successes and disappointments. Instantaneous feedback provides for the analysis which is immediately acted upon. Care must be taken not to allow ourselves even a moment of apathetic acceptance. Practicing focus and care is critical in order to develop the habitual expectation of success. A belief that may be lurking in the back of our mind for possible disaster can never seep into our consciousness. By adopting this rehearsal routine a professional commitment can foster the experience of playing our game as a result of perfect practice. The rehearsal begins to pre-condition our playing ability, allowing for the heightened expansion of understanding of the kinesthetic responses. Play now becomes less stressful and more natural. Our desire to continue the pursuit motivates a supporting passion for involvement. Although practicing is work, a total commitment to our process and the results that are derived are achieved with clarity of purpose. Work becomes play when our process is clearly defined. The pursuit now allows creative spirit to evolve, engaging our total life commitment.

Each experience in life offers the challenge to encounter a deeper insight into our character. If we begin to seek a truthful relationship to all of life's encounters, we will adopt an attitude that supports the commitment to playing like the pros. The acceptance of the rightness of our pursuits stands as an example that can serve as inspiration to others. We are each rewarded by our desire and willful capabilities to *pay it* forward as we *play it* forward. This sharing and compassion will be what finally defines our success in golf and life as we take the liberty to move forward in our pursuit of joy and infectious happiness that feeds our spirit. By fully engaging in all of life's experiences, we continually *go fore it* in all of our efforts and commitments. The content of character holds us true to whatever course we might encounter. Our ability to remain steadfast at the critical decisive moment of contact should mentally dismiss any past happenings whether positive or negative. As we continue to remain aware of the necessities, our purposeful connection to an unyielding pursuit as enthusiastic students of this game provides us with an explosive passion that lasts a lifetime.

Outcome of Effort

Anything in life that is worth pursuing requires a determined, passionate, purposeful effort that moves beyond the passing fancy of superficial involvement. Fundamental decisions to delve deep into any subject have a powerful effect on our self-concept. The outcome energizes our spiritual connection to the source of the commitment. The effort put forth in an attempt to overcome any deficiency in our ability or comprehension of the necessary fundamentals may not be immediately rewarded in apparent results. If we are strong-willed enough to overcome impatience, we can conquer weakness and frustration with the strength of our determined effort. We must not be turned away from the very involvement that provides the most inspiration to our life force. The decisions that we make to give in, give up, surrender, or persevere in spite of the difficulties finally define our true character. It all comes down to commitment to a purpose. As we evaluate the pursuit, we must look beyond the results achieved for the effort put forth. This is where our true strength of conviction lies.

When assurance runs high self-esteem supports our beliefs and allows for unparalleled moments of exhilaration. During these times we are in a state of absolute bliss as we discover the treasures of our existence. The accomplishment is accepted as the energy expended becomes realized. True success in life then transcends the shallow result of the immediate reward and shifts to the comprehension of the accepted output of effort. The final reward infinitely exists with a higher level of substance. Our self-realization now supports the recognition that is truly the result *of* and not the purpose *for* the pursuit. This understanding brings with it a sense of satisfaction that bypasses the weakness of the ego and goes directly to the heart and soul of divine nature.

When our willful intentions approach the higher ground of enlightened awareness, we are able to take on the tasks of our existence with grace and dignity. An ease of movement that produces effortless contact with whatever we are attempting to propel forward becomes our natural course of play. Justifiable pursuits will always connect to excellence when we are in alignment with the goals that we seek as long as they are not forced, but instead are nurtured from their basic, spiritual origin. It is the consistency of effort that determines the destination and becomes a meaningful part of our life's encounters. The final score will be recorded and justified without any subtraction for handicap. Effort put forth must become a manifestation of desired outcome. This is set into motion with effortless, graceful, rhythmic flow that is well timed, and well conceived. It becomes imperative that we channel our willful determination to reach the target without the imposition of any unintended beliefs that might negatively affect the outcome.

When we begin to accept the divine guidance that lies within our natural, intuitive being and recognize the aura of the force of our guiding light, we have moved a little closer to the infinite wisdom of the universal energy supporting our attempts. Present moments of creative pursuit provide the future possibilities that lie within the unveiling of the next opportunity as we prepare to rehearse for the game of life.

Past, Present, and Future

As I look back over the years of my passionate involvement, I realize that golf has evoked so many fine memories. As I sit at my writing table compiling these pages of thoughts on golf and its relativity to life's challenges, elations, disappointments, and redirections, I cannot help but contemplate where the game's course will lead me. Now, in my sixties, what inspiration could the game still provide in my life that I have not already experienced? What will the continued journey reveal? Although I never followed or realized my initial dream of becoming a tour player, I do not regret making a choice that would have taken my life in a totally different path. The direction and evolution of my game plan became clear as I thought about the path through my personal, divine guidance. I expanded my desire and ability to share the technical knowledge and psychological comprehension of the mental game. I believe that from the age of six, when Dad handed me that sawed off ladies brassie that he so carefully wrapped with electrical tape, I have been on a pre-determined course of purposeful pursuit.

Totally committed in my quest to share with others all that I have received, I have come to an understanding that it is not what we acquire and covet from our life's direction, but rather what those experiences have provided which motivate and inspire others through the determination of our sharing.

In the end we cannot take it with us, but we can certainly leave it behind in our legacy of devotion to our life and the lives of others. The writing of this book has provided a transformational encounter with a passion, purpose, process, and pursuit that carries on through the next thirty years of the continuing journey. Our play in life becomes more meaningful in the present with the efforts of execution, built on the past. Yet when we focus on the future reality, we accept the new vision presented with each stroke. If the intended purpose of the efforts within these pages is achieved, an example of what is possible will then be realized. If your game brings enjoyment and realization to become fully self-conceived and self-actualized, then the purpose of these present efforts are manifested in you, the recipient of the intended pursuit. The desire to *pay it* forward has been realized and accomplished. Born in the past, acted upon in the present, and projected into the future will complete the rehearsal for play.

Our efforts together become one of expansion that touches an eternal flow of energy for a future generation of players. This provides a creative, dynamic flow of positive goodness so necessary at this present time. The game of golf continues to endure, standing as an example of decency, honesty, integrity, and purposeful participation that exemplifies the conduct of life itself. At no time in history has there been a sport that has overtaken our imagination and provided an opportunity for recreation and camaraderie while still allowing *its* playful nature to carry us into our later life.

As I continue through my own aging process, I have chosen to live by example to others in my desire to achieve optimal health and wellness. While remaining focused on nutritional intervention and exercise, I strive to maintain the vitality necessary to carry out my life's mission. I welcome you to join me on this journey. What continues to penetrate the heart of my commitment is my personal concern for the well-being of all people I meet. My medium for expression as an artist of living life to the fullest is the offerings that lie at the core of the golfing experience. This connects our spirit to what *it* is that we are seeking in life. If we reflect on the past, live with determination and commitment in the present, then our future will be rewarded with unparalleled scoring ability. As we continue to rehearse for the next encounter within a mindful pursuit of our playful nature, we are able to hold true to uncompromising standards for excellence of effort.

The participants of today continue to have the privilege of involvement due to the commitment of those who have cleared the way through their absolute honesty and integrity. They stand as the examples that define the nature of what it is that inspires all who follow.

Chapter Eighteen

Game Play Standards

Historical Perspectives

It is difficult to imagine what *it* was that originally inspired the structure of the game of golf as we enjoy it today. There is no documented evidence of the first efforts in attempting to strike an inanimate object of any sort into a hole with the fewest number of attempts. Probably leisure time became the prime element that led our ancient ancestors to a desire to occupy time with frivolous activity. Once the challenges of basic survival were satisfied, their pursuits turned toward the need for expansion of basic human capacity as they acquired new skills and abilities. Creativity of the human spirit began to evolve and new ideas were born.

Probably controlled by the happenstance of the moment, someone for an unknown reason, decided to strike a sphere-shaped stone into a nearby hole in the ground. At that moment the realization of an intriguing process began to evolve and continued to progress. Through a motivated human desire the development of a simple premise became accepted as a fascinating way to occupy leisure time. The early inspiration for the game of golf was born. A simple idea that we are presented with in life can be picked up through the connected, potential meaning that we see in its purpose. A concept could have been perceived as meaningful and shared with other people or rejected as trite and unimportant for the support of human existence. It is just a matter of what decision was made and how much commitment it deserved. When confronted with an idea or concept that seems even remotely worthwhile do not question its validity. Why not just accept the possibilities and *go fore it?* When we examine the game of golf at its simplest state it begins to appear to be a bit of a miracle that it has ever evolved and grown into what it is today. If the game's potential was questioned golf may never have come into existence.

Documented evidence of the evolution of the game first appears during the time of Caesar. The Roman soldiers were said to have played a game called Paganica which utilized curved, wooden sticks to hit feather-filled leather balls, similar to the first golf balls. The Roman soldiers overran Europe and occupied Scotland and England in the fourth century, and most probably served to inspire the natives of these countries to develop the game of golf and claim it as their own. As mentioned earlier, the word golf is not an acronym for anything. It evolved from the Dutch word kolf or kolve which simply means club. In the later part of the fourteenth and early fifteenth centuries, the Scottish dialect took the Dutch word and created the word goff or gouff which changed in the sixteenth century to the word golf. They played kolf with a stick and ball on frozen canals in the winter. The Dutch sailors carried the game to the east coast of Scotland where it was played on public links land while continuing its evolution into the game we know today.

Golf has come a long way since those early days. It has become very technical through the evolution and development of superior clubs and golf balls. The courses have also become refined as the quality level continually improved. We are all very fortunate and privileged to participate in this involvement that has been carried down through the ages to the present time. It now becomes our responsibility to carry on the traditions. As we participate in this continuation of growth, we must adhere to and carry on the standards of play that have been laid down by those who have preceded us. The game of golf has taken on a momentum that allows for its evolution to expand. The participants of today continue to have the privilege of involvement due to the commitment of those who have cleared the way through their absolute honesty and integrity. They stand as the examples that define the nature of what it is that inspires all who follow. As we continue to *go fore it,* let us pursue our efforts with an unyielding passion that establishes a clarity of purpose. This in turn can define a process of perpetual growth. The pursuit of any endeavor that is supported by a cornerstone of high values serves as an example and provides the life force that leads us forward as we achieve our final reward.

For the Good of the Game

As golf became more formalized it was apparent that decisions on standardized play must be uniform to avoid conflicting opinions that may arise from some unforeseen situations or circumstances. In 1744 The Honorable Company of Edinburgh Golfers laid down the official rules to govern play for the first formal competition. The annual challenge for the silver club competition set the initial standards for competitive play. Originally, there were only thirteen rules. Today, the rules of golf are so complex and extensive that they could overwhelm the average player. This is probably why rules officials are available on the course for any necessary interpretations or decisions during some amateur and all professional tournaments.

Return with me for a moment to 1744. Pull up your knee socks, put on your knickers, and let us digest these original rules of golf. Notice should be taken of the unusual language of the time when the first rules of play were established.

1. **You must tee the ball within a club's length of the hole just completed.**
   Can you imagine what the greens looked like back in those days? Now we are concerned with ball marks and wear soft spikes, using care not to scuff our feet. Back then, you might have had to contend with a divot somewhere on the green resulting from a previous player's tee shot.

2. **Your tee must be on the ground.**
   The tees in those days were small, pyramid formed piles of wet sand located on the ground, but where else would they be found? Today tees are formed in a variety of shapes, lengths, and are constructed from varying materials. Wouldn't you

have liked to have the patent on the development of the first wooden tee?

3. **You are not to change the ball which you strike off the tee.**

   Golf balls of that time were not structured with the durability of today's technology. Damage to the ball's construction in those days was very possible, however the playability of the ball probably would not have been a problem on such poorly manicured greens.

4. **You are not to remove stones, bones, or any break club, except upon fair green and that only within a club's length of the ball.**

   Can you imagine how concerned the maintenance crews eye for detail might have been if players were concerned with animal bones and discarded clubs?

5. **If your ball comes among water or any watery filth, you are at liberty to take out your ball and bringing it behind the hazard and teeing it, you may play it with any club and allow your adversary a stroke for so getting out your ball.**

   Wouldn't it be nice nowadays to tee up the ball after going in the water?

6. **If your balls be found anywhere touching one another, you are to lift the first ball till you play the last.**

   I have decided to withhold comment on this rule. I hope you understand why.

7. **At holing you are to play your ball honestly at the hole and not play upon your adversary's ball, not lying in your way to the hole.**

   There could have been some confusion with cricket or billiards during these days. Back then, the game was played with stymies, which means that one ball is in the same line as another player's ball. The players were not allowed to mark their position and remove the ball as we can today.

Therefore, it became necessary to chip over your opponent's golf ball to advance to the hole even if this occurred on the green.

8. **If you should lose your ball, by its being taken up, or any other way, you are to go back to the spot where you struck last and drop another ball and allow your adversary a stroke for the misfortune.**

   In today's lingo, this means one stroke and distance for a lost ball. When in doubt, a good rule of thumb is to always consider playing a provisional ball.

9. **No man at holing his ball is to be allowed to mark his way to the hole with his club or anything else.**

   Considering how rough the putting surfaces must have been back then I am not sure this really would have mattered.

10. **If a ball be stopped by any person, horse, dog, or anything else, the ball so stopped must be played where it lies.**

    Judging by this rule, golf courses must have been quite open to animal intrusion.

11. **If you draw your club in order to strike and proceed so far in the stroke as to be bring down your club, if then your club should break in any way, it is to be accounted as a stroke.**

    Obviously there was not much to be said for the structural quality of the technology of those days. Hickory shafts are not recommended for today's players, however there are many rules today governing the exact allowable specifics of both golf clubs and balls.

12. **He whose ball lies farthest from the hole is obliged to play first.**

    This does not differ from today's rule and actually seems somewhat normal.

13. **Neither trench, ditch, or dyke made for the preservation of the links, nor the scholar's holes or the soldier's line**

shall be accounted a hazard but the ball is to be taken out, teed and played with any iron club.
It sounds like the game was played on a true battlefield of competition.

Today's rules are extensive and must take into consideration all contingencies. It is imperative to understand the basic rules of play and certainly when in competition act with the highest level of honesty and integrity. When just beginning the game or when playing for recreation, feel free to take liberties. Be aware however, when you are in violation of the rules and please ask the Golf Gods for forgiveness. Explain to them that you are cheating for the reason of reducing an already stressful experience. Remember to enjoy yourself as you learn the game. After you are adequately capable, then play by the rules and be true to yourself.

Code of Conduct

While the rules of golf must exist to provide guidance for fairness of play, conscious awareness of how we conduct ourselves should become a significant part of a respectful acceptance of behavioral standards. Golf etiquette has developed over the years and has been standardized into categories of prescribed, appropriate behavior. These recognized requirements should appeal to the player as common sense. However, through my years of playing, I have come to realize the need for occasional, gentle reminders. These are necessary to protect the game from the disrespect that periodically interferes with the overall enjoyment for all players. I feel that it is important enough to highlight and document some of the most significant of these standards within the context of this book. I can only hope that it will be preserved as a reference and reminder for you in the years to come.

I open to these considerations first and foremost with the care of the course of play. When divots are taken in the process of playing a stroke, they should be replaced whenever possible. When coming upon another player's divot left dislodged, replacing it provides you with a sense of dignified pride for which the Golf Gods will bless you. In like manner, bunkers should be raked properly and ball marks on the greens should be repaired. Keep a divot tool handy in your pocket for this purpose.

Take the time to pick up trash left by those who are less considerate. I strongly believe that we must leave the golf course in better condition than we found it.

Speed of play is also a major consideration that cognitively requires our focus and attention. The interesting element here is that it is not how well a person plays or how far they hit their shot that presents the problem. It has more to do with wasted time between strokes. It is important to walk at a reasonable pace and, when finishing a hole, to clear the green quickly. Always attempt to keep up with the group in front of you and when you fall behind, consider allowing other players the option to play through. It also is important to limit your practice swings. Consider that you might be wasting your best swing of the day. You should establish a pre-shot routine and then do not deviate from it.

Safety on the golf course is of absolute importance. Always be aware of the location of your playing partners before you decide to take a practice swing. The safest position to be in is facing the player who is executing a stroke— never behind, in back of, and of course in front of that player. If your ball is headed toward another player, always sound the loudest alert of *fore*! This is the traditional warning recognized by golfers as a shortened version to beware before you get hit.

One of the most disturbing behaviors periodically observed on the golf course is an outburst of anger or frustration. These are rude, childish, and unwelcome in this time-honored game. You should not allow this unacceptable attitude to affect your game or that of your playing partners with this purposeless, inappropriate behavior. Other players' opinions of you will diminish progressively until no one wants to accompany you on your round of golf.

The highest level of respect should be shown upon reaching the green. Always remain aware of other players' positions and avoid walking on their intended line of play. If your position is in their path, you should carefully mark your ball with an unobtrusive marker, such as a small coin. When removing the flag, loosen it carefully so as not to dislodge the cup and lay it down gently on the green, away from other players' golf balls. Do not allow your shadow to cross the line of another player's position and always clear the green upon completion. Record your score after leaving the putting surface, which allows anyone behind you to hit their approach shot to the green.

At the end of every round, shake hands with your fellow players, congratulating the ones who have played well and consol those who did not. At the end of the day, remember that the great pleasure is the time spent with friends of the game.

Finally, it is important to note that the game of golf has always adhered to an unofficial dress code. At one time, men wore jackets and ties and ladies wore dresses. Although it has become more relaxed, a player should always try to look their best. If you observe the standards demonstrated by the men and women who play golf for a living, you will most likely fit into the comfort of proper appearance. When you look your best, it can have a very positive effect on your entire persona that, in turn, inspires your best efforts. The standards we hold ourselves to as we participate in our game play demonstrates who we are as individuals, what we represent, and stand for in all of our life's pursuit.

Doctrine of Decision

Equally important to understanding and playing by the rules and proper etiquette is the personal standard for the expanded effort of our *play ability*. The decision to move forward in a desire for higher levels of achievement becomes a major supporting factor to our individual self-concept. A chosen direction requires a structural guidance system of clearly defined requirements and a plan of action. This plan is related to goal setting and accountability, but goes a little deeper and calls upon a basic value system within the cornerstone of our beliefs. When the development is motivated by determination to achieve higher proficiency in our game play, then we are able to remain true to a fundamental choice achieving whatever we decide to pursue. The clarity of purpose has a doctrine of decisive action that supports our absolutely dedicated efforts. This course of action greatly aids in the ongoing renewal of a passionate involvement in whatever we are attempting in golf and all of our endeavors in life.

In the process of designing a doctrine, we should adhere to a structure that aligns with the fundamental values within the game. Every round of golf we play is looked upon as an adventure, as well as an exploration into a deeper comprehension of what *it's* all about. If we begin to accept the game's intrigue in this manner, we open ourselves to a realization of the calm, quiet, solitude presented to us through the beauty of the course's environment. As we meld into this harmonious connection, a playful freedom of response provides an inner peace that can evoke the commitment to challenge the trust in our competence. Decisive actions support a positive attitude of self-reliance. This becomes necessary to establish the accountability of acceptable play both in discipline and perseverance. We then are assured of our progress in an efficient manner. If we honor the independence that is achieved with a spirit of gratitude and integrity, then our doctrine of decisiveness becomes the rule of law. This establishes a tradition of personal growth through a pursuit of excellence that opens our creative potential. The quality of the effort inspires the goodwill and friendship of our playing partners while giving back a truthful dedication to the wisdom of tolerant behavior. Our success and that of others endures as the respect and concern for each other's well-being is unified in a mutual enjoyment and pursuit.

We must be realigned in a determined desire that supports a decision to reach for the expansion of our capability. Pursuit should not be for the satisfaction of ego fulfillment, but rather the overall good of our game. We then expect to achieve at a heightened *play ability* that connects a spiritual sensibility to our purpose. Determination to progress happens when the requirements of our needs become evident. *Going fore it* is now a part of the natural evolution within the flow zone of our existence.

Winning Ways

Striving to achieve at higher levels of efficiency and capability must remain in balance with our purpose. It is very easy at times to get caught up in the momentum of determined effort driven by a desire to be the best we can be. We easily lose sight of the reasons for the pursuit that originally motivated and inspired us at the outset of our journey. The desire to win overcomes the passion to participate. Winning is accomplished easily when a heartfelt connection to the task is moved by meaningful acceptance of capability produced by our efforts.

I counsel quite carefully to assist my students in their realization of the small steps, or as I like to refer to them, as the small trophies in their accomplishments. Each of these victories can stand by themselves and do not tarnish over time. These advancements also construct the support system that bears the disappointment with each attempt to achieve perfection. As they begin to connect to the importance of the acceptance and alignment of natural growth in their ability, they become patient with the required diligence of a purposeful pursuit. When results are achieved, they are internalized within a strength of beliefs that allows for the effortless flow of instinctive understanding.

Each required circumstance is accomplished and becomes instantly recognized and utilized in a responsive, executed effort, void of overexertion of desire. In short, we exist in the flow zone of our being. Recognizing the depths of our oneness, we are able to move away from the superficial concerns that occupy our consciousness. As we begin to connect to the transcendent force of spiritual awakening, we are enabled to achieve a higher state of awareness. We are now in proper alignment to commit to the ongoing pursuit, opening our journey to the unexpected encounters that further expand a depth of focus. Future goals are revealed to us within the present moment of achievement and motivate our intent to move on to the next step on an infinite path of existence. The knowledge we have gained serves as the recognized victory presented through a process of self-realized, spiritual connection to the true meaning and purpose of the winning pursuit.

There is no trophy that can be presented that glimmers brighter in the mind's eye of our memory. This stands as solid as the simplicity of achievement, even in the smallest task of resistance that has been endured and overcome. The ability to continually rise to the occasion as we face our difficulties and overcome the challenge of adversity provides the ultimate strength of conviction. We now are led to the fulfillment of our final, victorious moments. Once we have recognized the necessity of maintaining high standards of personal expectation of our potential, we take full credit for the journey's accomplishment. Efforts are not spent for satisfaction of ego, but for the grateful acceptance of the rewards received by the strength of the spiritual connection to the force that we encounter. Our standards that we hold true provide the final trophy that recognizes the continuance of our winning ways.

To achieve consistency of contact, we must develop a sensibility that allows for a fluid motion, which coordinates all parts of the body in a seamless, coordinated movement creating maximum club head speed at impact.

Chapter Nineteen

Play Ability

Swinging Away

Gaining a comprehensive understanding of how to play the game of golf is most appropriately accomplished through contact with an experienced golf instructor. Much of the learning process requires a demonstration that can be visually captured and transferred to the student. Written or pure verbal explanations often can fall short and are easily misinterpreted. However, I would be remiss if I did not share some of the thought processes that I have advocated over my years of teaching. I attempt to effectively simplify and transfer an understanding of the fundamental processes that inspire and motivate my students' commitment to the active pursuit of the game's technical requirements.

First, let me begin with one of the most neglected, yet most important parts of the golf swing, the pre-shot routine. This was covered previously, but I would like to review the process here in relationship to the full swing. Every serious player should have a definite pattern of approaching each shot. I am providing a suggested process that is modified as experience is gained. Initially, this establishes a framework to develop a procedure to follow.

As we are approaching the first tee, let us assume that a driver has been selected as the club of choice. Begin by positioning yourself six to ten feet behind the teed ball. The height of the tee is a personal preference and should be adjusted as conditions require. Start by taking one or two practice swings to get the feel of your body mechanics in relationship to the club head and the target line. Now, standing directly behind the ball, look down the line of flight and imagine the intended trajectory toward the target. Approach the golf ball while continuing to keep the line in your mind's eye. Position the clubface perpendicular to the line of flight. This is referred to as a square position. Now, set your feet perpendicular to the line of flight with the ball positioned off the inside of the left heel. Different clubs require varying ball positions so feel free to adjust as necessary. Your toes should be pointed out slightly for better balance. Check the distance from your toes to the imaginary line of flight. They should be equidistance. Some adjustment may be necessary, but this is adequate in the beginning. I am assuming now that you have a basic understanding of the grip. There are a variety of different grips to try, but in the beginning, I would recommend a ten-finger grip for better control. When your swing becomes more consistent, then you can try different variations of hand positions.

To set your posture, stand up straight and drop your arms down naturally to full extension. Your arms will not allow the club to reach all the way down to the ground, so just allow them to relax. By bending forward at the hips, your upper body now permits the club to rest on the ground. Your hands are in position directly under your head. The club is at the appropriate distance from your body. The ball should be played forward toward your left foot. This position allows for proper release through to your intended target. Keep your head and neck in alignment with your back, which maintains your spine angle. Now recheck your alignment. At this point, we need to create a relaxation response. Proceed by simply taking a deep breath and exhaling slowly while saying in your head a relaxing thought like, *let it go*. The goal here is to bring our mind, body, and spirit into a quiet, meditative state of mindful mindlessness, just before we start the take away of the swing.

With the completion of a good pre-shot routine and proper set up, we are now ready for takeaway and backswing. This part of the swing is most critical. It sets up the width of the swing arc, puts the body into a dynamic balance, and sets up the process of proper rhythm and tempo allowing for the development of proper timing. As movement away from the ball position begins, the club head should come back slowly—

remaining low to the ground. Attention to body movement should be on the shoulder turn as the arms move back. Care must be taken not to break the wrists too quickly. The grip should be light, as if you are holding a baby bird or a raw egg. Avoid squeezing the club tightly, which allows the hands a softer, more supple feel. This method promotes a smoother back swing, which permits the club to move away from the ball on a path inside the target line. When the club reaches halfway back or belt height, its face should be pointing in a straight upward direction. The shaft should be parallel to the ground and aligning with the intended ball flight. This is a good checkpoint. The backswing then continues to the top of the swing arc in an unhurried manner with gradual acceleration to the top. Continue the shoulder turn until it reaches 180 degrees to the ground plane. This may be restricted due to lack of flexibility and is different for every golfer. As the club choice progresses from the wedge through the driver, the backswing naturally gets increasingly longer. At the top of the backswing there is a very slight pause. The club head at this position should be pointing down the line of flight with the face parallel to the target line. Now that a good backswing has been completed, we are prepared for an unhurried downswing.

When the club is properly positioned at the top the backswing, the progression should be carried out in a rhythmic, effortless motion allowing the club to closely reverse the path on the downswing. The tendency people have is to either swing down quickly or with too much force. Any impatient move from the top of the swing causes the club to move out and away from the proper swing plane. The path of the club moves from the outside to the inside of the line of flight. This movement shifts the weight of the body out of position creating a tendency to fall back as the body opens up. This restricts the rotation of the club face that permits it to square at impact. The entire problem is alleviated by developing an unhurried downswing that allows the club to swing on the proper plane. Powerful contact is not the result of a forceful swing, instead it is the outcome produced by a series of levers. This lever action produces club head speed that is created by shoulder turn, arm and wrist release, leg drive, and weight shift all connecting at the moment of impact in a perfectly timed and coordinated motion.

The arms are freed as the left hip clears the way for a proper downswing setting up a full extension through the ball. The head and body are allowed to come up naturally and the weight fully shifts to the left side. An unhurried process permits for a very natural follow through. Holding the finish is not necessary, but may be helpful at first for certainty of achieving the intended result. Obviously, all relationship to right and left would be reversed for the left-handed players. Connecting these suggested references to the mechanics with rhythm, timing, tempo, and a relaxed attitude provides the structure for a positive outcome.

Philosophy of Flow

Becoming a good ball striker is more than mastering the basic mechanics of the swing that has been covered thus far. We are consistently challenged to make adjustments in search of a better result. To achieve consistency of contact, we must develop a sensibility that allows for a fluid motion, which coordinates all parts of the body in a seamless, coordinated movement creating maximum club head speed at impact. This is what we call *feel*. This attitude that lurks within the mind, coupled with the combined construct of rhythm, tempo, and timing, work in concert to produce this quality of flow. Our body, mind, and spirit must be in proper balance in executing every swing from the booming tee shot down to the more delicate three inch putt. To achieve this, our mind-set must be openly accepting and aware of the process while at peace with the requirements of the intended result. Wanting desire for success must yield to the intuitive sensibility of process as we pursue our goal with passionate determination for the connection to the purpose.

Once again, we return to this premise that serves us well in our quest for achieving anything in life. To analyze how these elements of a fluid golf swing connect, I suggest a methodology that is adaptable to the requirements of solid ball striking. When we understand and have had reasonable success with the development of a swing that is generated from shoulder turn rather than arm and hand control, we are prepared to apply an acceptance of rhythm, timing, and tempo. These three aspects, when joined with an attitude that is not imposing on our strong willful desire to control results, allows for the proper development of a psychological acceptance of the ease of flow that we seek.

Through my studies in Eastern philosophy and meditation, I have discovered a process that helps us create a repeatable, effortless motion in our swing. This procedure automatically coordinates the levers of shoulders, hips, legs, arms, wrists, and hands, which allow for the consistency we are trying to achieve. As we pursue the connection that is desired, we cannot let a constant flood of indecisive thoughts overtake our deliberate actions. We must find a method of putting the brain at rest in an accepting manner, rather than an all-controlling one. We have an opportunity to learn how to elicit a peaceful state of non-controlling flow when we call upon some of the methods used in meditative practices.

Starting with the breathing process mentioned earlier, we see ourselves at address position open to the starting point of the swing. If, from this point, we could hold onto a specific rhythm count as the swing proceeds, our body movement falls into a pattern of motion that can be automatically coordinated. The mind could then stop its desire to make momentary judgments during the process of the swing. The complete movement is timed in a three count structure related to the take away on one, top of the back swing on two, and the downswing and follow through on three. This three count assures a slower backswing and a continual acceleration down from the top, through impact, on to the extension and follow through. Going one step further, I have found that if I utilize specific words that relate to the process of the swing, I can create a mantra that effectively programs the subconscious mind and thereby produces the proper timing of a repetitive swing. I suggest the word *back* for the one-count, which describes and creates a command for proper takeaway and backswing. At the top of the swing, we say to ourselves the word *and* for the transition position on the two count. The down swing and extension beyond the ball position utilizes the word *through* which suggests hitting through the ball, rather than *at* the ball, as so many players mistakenly believe is necessary. Once the player is able to internalize this approach, a rhythmic efficiency that produces consistent results has a profound effect on a repeatable outcome. Beginner and advanced students alike see significant improvement utilizing this procedure.

Having a consistent process in the pursuit of any endeavor always provides the structural support that we need for a belief systems to accept our capability. Self-doubt is overcome in accordance with what psychology accepts in the consistency of our performance. Flow in life is achievable if the methods are put into proper alignment with desired intentions of clear purpose. As we continue a properly manifested pursuit of success, we are assured that the passion for golf, life, and living promotes longevity through effortless, flowing motion.

Approaching the Green

Without question the heart of the game of golf lies from 150 yards out from the green to the final tap in. You achieve an ease of *play ability* with consistent practice of the variety of strokes necessary to accomplish a reasonable level of proficiency. The short game is almost a game unto itself. It is a part of the game that the recreational golfer can develop to a rather high level of proficiency with minimal practice, if they gain comprehensive understanding of the fundamental concepts. A good short game player has an instinctive feel for distance. The backswing determines how much effort is required from varying positions related to the distance from the hole. We all have this instinctive ability within us, but it has not been allowed to properly develop.

Although the short game can be defined from 150 yards from the green, this aspect of our game becomes most critical when we get to a distance where the required shot is less than a full swing. At this point in the game a sense of touch is required. This calls upon the instinctive sense that we all possess within us. As we become familiar with the various distance requirements, we begin to develop a felt response to the three-quarter, half, and one-quarter swing. Accuracy is now the goal of our pursuit, not distance. This requires a precise, but simplified methodology that is carefully constructed to produce an easily repeatable pattern in the stroke. It becomes imperative that the ball is hit on a descending angle of intent avoiding the subconscious desire to scoop the ball off the turf.

To set up for the pitch shot, we should open our stance which allows the body to set slightly to the left of the target line. This position leads to a feeling for distance and directional control that aids in the natural touch that eventually is developed. The condition of the green and whether it is sloping toward or away from the fairway determines how much backspin you might want to impart on the ball. Experimenting with ball position in relation to the center of your stance at set up enables you to gain control of how much roll the ball has after hitting the putting surface. The further the ball is played back in the stance, the greater the amount of spin. This shot requires experimentation and patience, but with practice and commitment you learn to develop a masterful ability to accomplish this desired outcome.

As we approach the putting surface, precision of setup and activation of our intuition becomes more critical. Getting closer to the green our stance should open up more to the line of flight. This is accomplished by turning our body more to the left of the target. The feet get a little closer together, minimizing our balance and causing our body to remain still. This is necessary for the steadying of body motion as it produces an improved chance of making perfectly square contact with the ball. With the shorter pitch shot, I recommend a movement at address, immediately before the beginning of the backswing, which is referred to as a forward press. The mechanics of this technique are quite easy to learn. At address, the hands should be in alignment with the ball. The first position required should allow the hands to move toward the hole about two to four inches. This movement sets the hands in the proper relationship to the ball at address. The simplified position created by this technique of the swing eliminates the necessity for breaking the wrists as the arms swing the club back which could cause an inconsistency in the angle of the club at impact. The backswing can now continue its motion from the forward press. The club face must remain square to the intended line of flight, neither turned in nor out. There should not be any additional wrist break on the backswing. The downswing starts in an unhurried fashion, maintaining the wrist position through impact and follow through. It is imperative that the wrists maintain their position through the furthest point of the follow through. This technique produces a crisp contact with the ball and causes it to check and sit down quickly as it rolls toward the target, reducing the tendency to jump left or right. If we work on this technique diligently, a great sense of satisfaction is derived in building a self-realized confidence in our short game play.

At the root of any involvement, there is nothing that serves us better than acquiring a comprehensive understanding of what is needed to accomplish our desired outcome. The methods that have been described thus far assure a successful result if practiced diligently. When we are fortunate enough in life to discover a methodology that stimulates our creative instinct to a point where we can pursue it with passion, then there is nothing that can possibly alter our directional course of purposeful play. We are now free and unhindered in achieving even our wildest dreams. I believe that this is the essence that lies within the spirit of golf that inspires so many to experience what *it* is that golf offers to the quality of our lives.

Bunker Blues

Becoming a true student of the game requires a comprehensive study of all aspects of play. One of the least understood parts of golf lies in the sand of the fairway and greenside bunkers. Nothing spoils a day's enjoyment more than two or three extra strokes as we attempt to recover from the errant shots that find the sand. In observing bunker play over the years, I rarely see the proper technique used in what appears to be a futile effort of survival to just get out of a bunker. We must learn to achieve reasonable control to get close enough to the hole to be able to one putt, perhaps even saving par. Many times the effort of the player results in a thinly hit shot that sails over the green and requires additional recovery shots. In an effort to avoid such disaster, the player might dig deep into the sand and leave the ball still sitting unmoved or even now buried completely. Taking time to seek proper instruction on methodology here is absolutely essential.

The sand shot is all about proper technique and turns out to be one of the easiest shots in golf. Most of the methods of successful bunker play lie in the set up. In order to be properly positioned, the player must have a clear *sense ability* of relation to the line of flight. The club face needs to be set square to the line of flight. While maintaining this position, the player aligns their body open to the target. This is similar to the short pitch shot. It should feel as though the body placement is aiming left of the target in this open position. The actual swing arc is maintained parallel to the body line. The ball is played off the inside of the left heel so that when the stroke is played, the bounce of the club through the sand will propel the ball from its position with the force of the sand. The club face never actually comes in contact with the ball. This technique impacts significant backspin on the golf ball, allowing it to land softly on the green with a slight release toward the intended target. With a little practice, this technique can be easily achieved, while saving strokes and providing greater inspiration and satisfaction.

The fairway bunker is quite a different story. In this shot, the player must make a very precise impact on the ball prior to any contact with the sand. It is really no different than hitting off the fairway except that the lower body must remain more stable to avoid slipping in the loose footing of the sand base. Digging the feet in slightly can help significantly in stabilizing the body to support the efforts of the swing. It is usually advisable to choke down a little on the club for control and feel, as well as to compensate for the inch or so of a lower body position, caused by your feet settling down into the sand. The actual swing should be made with increased awareness of proper rhythm. Smoothness of the stroke is the critical component of all sand play.

As with every aspect of the game, continued practice is required to accomplish the desired technique. The basis for all achievement in life is a connection with and commitment to the four fundamental components of human capability of expansion, which lie within the continuum of the passionate, purposeful, process of our pursuit.

On the Putting Surface

A player's game from the edge of the green to the hole is without a question the most important aspect of golf and is responsible for approximately half of the strokes taken on the course by most average players. Yet, it is the least practiced and in most cases the least taught. Putting is a game unto itself. Individual preferences of style include stance, grip, putter types, and stroke, which are all open to experimentation. There are, however, certain fundamentals that should be considered if consistency is to be achieved.

The two main objectives in accomplishing the goal of consistency are direction, structured by proper alignment, and distance control, which is developed through experience that provides a sensibility of touch.

Directional position is created by the ability of the player to understand the line of the putt in relationship to the squareness of the putter blade. Regardless of how well the line is determined, if the putter face comes into contact with the ball, somewhat open or slightly closed, the outcome of the putt will be significantly affected. The result causes a potential miss to the left or right of the hole. However, the blade must remain perpendicular to the intended line of the putt. As you practice, it is necessary to work diligently to deliver the putter square on the line toward the hole, while taking the undulations of the green into consideration. The nature and quality of the stroke becomes the critical component that must be rehearsed until it is automatic. Feel for the break of the green is acquired through experience.

There are basically two types of strokes that can be used when putting. In the first, the putter is brought away from the ball square on the intended line, and then returns back on the extended path precisely toward the hole. In the second type of stroke the putter is brought back on the inside of the line away from the hole. It then returns back to the ball making square contact, while continuing through and allowing for proper release on the target line. This method seems more natural and easy to achieve, although I have found it to be less accurate than a movement that remains square throughout the stroke.

Consistency in putting seems to be most dependent on the smoothness of movement back and through the ball. This is achieved by developing a continuity of rhythmic, flowing motion. The methodology that I have found to be the most effective is conceptualized by imagining the putter to be the pendulum of a grandfather's clock. By visualizing the movement of the pendulum and associating the rhythm of the putter swing to a one-second cadence of the tick tock sound, we are able to superimpose a consistency of movement that provides a control for speed and distance. As we make the stroke, we create a meditative moment by reciting to ourselves a tick, while taking the putter back, and a tock as the putter moves through on the intended line. This method assures proper execution of each stroke. With a little practice, you will experience remarkable results as the tick tock mantra is consistently repeated.

Golf provides a very special opportunity that combines the science of physics with the art of poetry, while adding a touch of sensibility that evokes the spiritual essence of the depth of our divine human nature. Many times our day's experience comes down to the short tap in putt. All of the suggestions that have been provided up to this point come down to the spiritual satisfaction of the disappearance of the ball into the bottom of the cup. This energizes the continued pursuit of our game. We remain true to proper alignment and expand our intuition to a point in which we trust the instinctive sense of flow. Then, we can gain the ability to move through life with the ease and grace of forward momentum, captured within the natural body rhythm. This holds true in most of our playful ability in golf and life.

For in the end it's only a game—but what a game it really is.

Chapter Twenty

Well-being

Life Pursuit

To feel fully alive we must seek and discover a central motivating force that not only requires, but also demands, our fully committed efforts. When this is achieved, we are able to tap an energy source that inspires the creative resources through a divine guidance. This guiding force continues to infuse our passionate commitment that we hold in our illuminated vision of possibilities. The dreams that are the cornerstones and support the structure of the pursuits in life are filled by a human value system as we are gently led on the journey to our fully self-realized potential. The rewards of the achievements are recognized by our spiritual renewal, rather than an ego-filled acquisition of materialistic gain. All that is necessary comes to us in an effortless flow of a life response as our purpose is defined and the process enables the determination and tenacity to carry on an infinite pursuit. Our life's journey then has the potential to continue on to be an inspiration to all those who follow.

When we discover the power that lies within us through a well-defined purpose, we look forward to constantly attracting good fortune. At times, it descends upon us in the surprise ah-ha moment of sudden realization, seemingly from parts unknown. This is the release of our instinctive, intuitive sensibility that we must learn to accept and trust.

When we become aligned in this fashion, miracle-like experiences surface with limited effort within the realm of our reality. By learning to activate the positive force of attraction, whatever we intend to accomplish easily comes to pass. Life experiences and circumstances are guided by the inner trust of our capacity to endure the challenges that are bound to interfere. Difficulties just seem to melt away and reveal true opportunities as our mundane routines become exhilarating moments of expanded awareness. Now we are energized by faith in our self-realized beliefs.

As we continue to develop in this process, we gain a sense of calm harmony with the experiences of life. We seem to just know what to do and why we choose to do it. Our actions are guided as we learn to accept and trust them. Shielded from outside interference or infringement, our decisions seem to attract successful outcomes. The ability to gain knowledge through our process of insightful comprehension of the situation reveals a profound capability to make the right choices.

For our potential to be fully realized it is important to maintain a continuing desire to grow in capacity, allowing new and wondrous adventures into our life. The game of golf offers an intriguing pursuit that provides an involvement away from our everyday activities. Challenging encounters on the course effectively satisfy the desire we have to expand our psychological, physical, and spiritual capabilities. We gain a sense of wholeness in our well-being from the fundamentals of the mind, body, and spirit trilogy as they interconnect with every successful stroke we take. Each round of golf inspires a passionate involvement through the joy-filled moments of exhilaration. The intuitive revelations of our encounters should be cherished as a deeper meaning promotes a desire to continue onward in our commitment to life, both on and off the course. A well-being will be energized by the day-to-day choices that offer us the opportunities supporting a desire to pursue life to our full capacity.

Forever Young

The influences that we have been conditioned by have a defining effect on what we believe to be our state of well-being. What we choose to accept and reject provides the influential guidance that determines the eventual outcome in our development. As life experience continues to unfold, a process of self-realization opens to a variety of encounters that challenge the course of life's journey. We have the opportunity to take those paths that offer the least resistance or set our goals on higher levels of achievability. Challenging our capability and committing to a direction of action calls on a sensibility that stimulates a spiritual connection as we realize the excitement of possibilities that lie just beyond our reach. By maintaining a conscious, yet determined, awareness of possibilities to expand a state of existence, we are able to attain a forward momentum that supports our vitality and fuels a renewable energy source.

We have all seen people who have been dragged down by life's challenges; the passion has been sucked out of them by the acceptance of their circumstances. They become old before their time, often dying much too young. The unfortunate nature of their situations could have been reversed with just a simple change of thought. When we are able to attach ourselves to a purpose that we feel deserves time and attention, we make the necessary commitment to reignite a passion for life. This paradigm shift allows us to emphasize a forever young outlook of mind, body, and spirit. We have found our fountain of youth.

For me, *it* lies in the determined effort that has always been at the core of my being. I focus my intent on the commitment to have a positive influence on the lives of others. I have found that when I am able to move outside of my own needs and shift my focus to others, then all of my own life's requirements are more than satisfied. At the times in my life when I am on the brink of a new direction that could expand my capability to serve, I become most alive and vital in my own existence. Time begins to move at lightning speed. I can't wait to wake up to grasp the next day's opportunities and challenges. During these times, there is no sense of fatigue or lack of energy. My love of life and deep appreciation for each day provides the inspiration to maintain a healthy state of being through proper nutrition and exercise. This restores my energy and allows for the continuation of my pursuit.

Good fortune came into my life many years ago when my father first placed that women's brassie in my hands and allowed me to become involved with this magical game of golf. My life's pursuit of the wonders of the golfing experience has evolved into the central core of my motivation which I treasure and enjoy sharing. I am blessed that I am able to inspire my students to discover the youthful exhilaration within each of them. Well-being is vitally important to longevity and the ongoing commitment to giving, serving, and sharing. We all have a choice in life, so why not choose to be an inspiration to our fellow human beings? I hope you identify with this level of commitment that I have expressed within these pages and are motivated and inspired to live a life of youthful wonder. May you be physically, mentally, spiritually, and psychologically forever young.

Taking Care

Thanks to the game of golf I have gained a profound understanding of human nature within myself through playing, self-study, and my work with the many thousands of students that have come my way. The game has lifted me up in my determined desire to remain physically fit and healthy in order to enjoy the exhilaration that I experience in my teaching and playing. I now must work even more diligently to maintain a healthy existence, as I move into the last third of my life.

Everything the game provides was almost taken away from me fifteen years ago when I was told that I was suffering from coronary artery disease and required immediate quadruple bypass surgery. I was on the brink of a major, possibly fatal, heart attack. Even worse than that, it could have separated me from the reason for my existence, my lovely and wonderful wife, Beth. I accepted the challenge that shook the ground on which I walked. Beth and I faced life's adversity with a choice. Do we give into self-pity or to take charge and set a new game play for recovery? In the long run, this brush with death turned out to be one my greatest blessing.

Heart disease is an insidious, degenerative aliment that most times can be avoided with proper nutrition and a reasonable amount of exercise. An alarmingly high number of victims do not know they have a problem until their first heart attack, which could well be their last. I was one of the fortunate ones whose only symptom was fatigue. I must take a moment here to thank my personal physician, Dr. Arthur Klein, for his unwavering pursuit of a solution. If not for his care and the subsequent angiogram that revealed the severity of the problem, who knows what might have happened. I was referred to Valley Hospital in New Jersey and the talented hands of Dr. Bruce Mindich. Another grateful thanks must go out to all of the professionals at that facility for their saving grace.

My surgery took place on September 6, 1995. Normally, I would have been released in 3 or 4 days. However, I experienced complications that included a blood infection, collapsed lung, and excessive draining from my chest, which required four drain tubes to be left in my abdomen for eight days. An artery was removed from my left arm leaving an incision extending from my elbow to my wrist. This has become my constant visual reminder of what I do not want in my future. Whenever I glance down on this enormous scar, I recall my wife reminding me that my lifeline has been extended. Again, adversity became the motivator that helped me continue to take care of myself and do whatever is required to stay healthy and strong. I was in extreme discomfort for the first six weeks after the surgery, especially in my shoulders. I had particular concern because the shoulders are a key component in a well-formed golf swing. At two months after surgery, I was pretty well convinced that my life as a student and teacher of golf had come to an end. Even though depression was beginning to set in, I was not willing to accept it.

A year later, almost to the day, my wife and I joined our local Gold's Gym. I drastically changed my diet, although I must admit that I overreacted to a degree. I knew that I needed to make changes in both my eating habits and over-controlling nature. Fortunately, I discovered a class at a local hospital and began to study and practice a form of meditation, advocated by Deepak Chopra. He eventually became one of my mentors through his many books and lectures. Coincidentally, he has also taken up the game of golf. As mentioned previously, meditation has become a key component of my playing and teaching. This allows my students to develop a relaxation response that assists in relieving the desire to over-control outcome.

As the years have gone by, I now understand the importance of taking care of the God given capacities to be able to expand abilities in our chosen pursuits. Committing to well-being and reaching for a full potential, I enjoy the freeing, motivational force to *go fore it*. As a result of my personal misfortune and in a desire to offer further assistance to my students, I have become a certified life and health coach advocating proper nutrition and exercise. Both my wife and I now enjoy an optimal level of well-being and hope to continue our efforts of helping others on their personally designed course of existence. My pursuit in assisting others has once again fueled the passion and established a new and exciting purpose in life. Having an opportunity to evaluate, redesign, and restructure our pursuit provides a life force releasing the greatness that lies within. I strongly suggest that you choose to *go fore it.*

Physical Conditioning

Golf offers its participants a type of exercise that is enjoyed in a beautiful, tranquil environment that penetrates our soul and connects us to the marvels of nature. What better place to become centered within a motivating force that has the power to positively affect all of our life's pursuits? The game can be enjoyed at an even higher awareness with a properly conditioned body. The game itself requires a considerable amount of walking, even if a golf cart is used for assistance. The four to five mile walk that makes up a typical, full length golf course requires physical endurance. Therefore, it is advisable to participate in a regiment of aerobic exercise and resistance training. This helps to increase strength, stamina, and flexibility, as well as preventing injuries that interfere with our playing ability. Since my heart surgery, Beth and I have been regulars at the gym where we have access to all types of equipment, as well as a sizable indoor track and an Olympic-size pool. Although our sessions at the gym have been very helpful, I soon realized that there was something missing. As I've aged, I've found that I am beginning to lose the flexibility needed to execute a full body turn enabling me to produce power in my swing.

Strange, yet wonderful, things happen in our life response when a need is recognized. Last golfing season, I came into contact with a new student, Linda Yasek, who happens to be an exceptionally gifted Pilates trainer. Linda has since been working with me on flexibility and core strength training. I have also taken her on as a very serious golf student, whose passion for learning to play golf inspires my highest desires to teach. Our mutual efforts are leading us both in a new direction of physical, emotional, psychological, and spiritual wellness. I have become diligent and passionate about my Pilates training. This new awareness has offered me a method that helps to slow down the aging process and provides what is necessary to gain the longevity that my future plans require. In this transitional phase of my life, I am committed to a continuing effort of developing my concepts in playing and teaching through an expanded level of realization. It is only with the diligent care and maintenance of my physical capacity that I can completely appreciate all that I wish to accomplish.

Pilates is without a doubt one of the most efficient and effective methods of physical training available. Joseph Pilates, the creator of the methodology, was initially motivated by his own need to conquer his frailty as a child. Determined to become strong and healthy, he overcame his adversity and passionately dedicated himself to building his body, mind, and spirit through the practice of yoga, Zen meditation, as well as ancient Greek and Roman exercises. He became an accomplished gymnast, skier, boxer, and diver. It was not until his internment during World War II in England, for being a German citizen, that fate intervened and provided him with the inspiration for the beginning of the concept of the Pilates system.

Working as a nurse, he developed a method of assisting disabled patients to regain mobility and strength with an innovative process using springs and straps hooked onto hospital beds. His experimental treatment revealed a very clear process that developed recognition for the importance of core abdominal and back muscle strength. He found this provided stability to the torso allowing for freedom of movement. The discoveries he made working with his patients successfully led to creating the specialized equipment utilized in today's Pilates methods and the principles referred to as controlology. Joseph Pilates' pursuit led to the development of approximately 500 different exercises based on the principles of concentration, centering, flowing movement, and breathing that bring the mind, body, and spirit into alignment and promotes good health. Joseph Pilates died at age 87 from smoke inhalation in a studio fire. He hung from the rafters for over an hour, as he attempted to escape the flames. Unfortunately, he was ultimately consumed by the intense smoke.

After about twenty sessions of Pilates, I returned to the golf course this past summer, thanks to Linda's training, with a new sense of commitment to an expanded capability as a player and teacher. Through my discovery of Pilates, Linda and I can offer golf students a significant service to aid their overall capability. The potential of our combined efforts serves as another example of the life response that comes to the seeker. The passionate unveiling of clarity in the purpose, reveals the evolutionary process that allows for the facilitation of our pursuit. Joseph Pilates is a shining example of this life force to which we owe a debt of gratitude.

Wholeness

Life today seems to be increasingly more challenging and chaotic. The demands of jobs, families, and even our social interactions have created pressure sometimes causing an overwhelming state of anxiety. The ways and means by which we are able to remain aware and bring a sense of order to our daily schedules ultimately determine an efficiency and ease of movement. A change from our routine helps to achieve a sense of well-being. Fundamental peace of mind is maintained by the capability to keep our priorities in congruent alignment. The activities in which we participate should satisfy a need for rejuvenated realignment of our self-realized sense of flow. Adaptability to circumstances, that is, taking on each twist and turn of the ongoing journey, provides the precise catalyst for creative adventure. Designing clear goals and objectives has the potential to produce the sense of well-being that we seek. If we plan carefully, it is possible to bring an effective, orderly balance to the demands of our daily existence. Overall health and happiness are dependent on a determined intent to pursue this course of committed effort. If we do not attend to the proper support of our game play in golf, as well as life, it will control us.

Each day when we go out on the golf course, we witness a direct correlation to our life's experience. So much can be learned from the game that applies to daily encounters off the course. If we find a way to be more playful in our participation, we will discover a method of organization and structure aligning with whatever we encounter along the way. Our process then evolves out of necessity, rather than a desire to superimpose immediate, reactionary, willful control. Achieving well-being that comes with the acceptance of circumstance allows us to realize the *response ability* that supports a sense of self-worth. Overall well-being is dependent upon conditional acceptance of our decisive actions in response to the situations that arise. Decisions that are made in a reactive moment of anxiety, fear of failure, or despair can throw our psychological stability out of balance and create significant self-doubt. This state of being produces a chain reaction of negative results in all of our efforts going forward. This is not permanent, but can leave an indelible imprint that flashes back at the most uncontrollable moments. We must remember the power of the subconscious mind.

The consistency with which we are able to place our mental state in a relaxed and peaceful place allows for the graceful sense of flowing motion that we search for in our movement through life. The challenges remain and the frustrations, disappointments, and even disastrous outcomes disrupt our desired path. They cannot be totally avoided. We can, however, learn to make choices in our game play that position us at a more stable and predictable point of expectation of the results that we seek. Through consistent, proper planning on the courses of golf and life, we have the ability to establish a sense of well-being in our pursuits as true students of our game. Consistently *going fore it*, free from fear and anxiety, becomes our way of life.

Final Words

The decision to finally take on the task of putting together a lifetime of thoughts, reflections, memories, and realizations has been an experience for me that I will cherish for the rest of my life. I am the first to admit to a lack of literary mastery that may show in the structure of my words and phrases. I hope, however, that you, the reader, are able to transcend any inadequacies that lie within the text and accept my authentic desire to share my revelations in my pursuit of golf and life.

I have always tried to be very realistic about my abilities and remain unthreatened by any concern for ego fulfillment. This characteristic is what has freed my spirit. I have achieved a natural ability to accept both success and failure simply as the way of things. Because of this, I have been able to identify a strong purpose that has been connected by my passion to share what I have learned with other human beings in a well-defined intent that motivates and inspires. As I teach the game, I am always on a cooperative, parallel journey with my inquiring students. I learn as much as I teach. My instructional methods may seem strange at times, but spontaneity has provided me with an ability that allows for an interaction with my students that removes all unnecessary inhibitions. The thoughts and actions are autonomous and independent of conventional dictates. The ethical nature of the process remains self-actualized and is determined by the divine guidance of a universal energy source.

As participants in the game of golf, we together accept our inadequacies while always playing to the best of our ever evolving capabilities. This provides us with the satisfaction of continued growth while graciously accepting our current levels of achievement. When play brings us an adventurous excitement and exhilaration, our spirit is rejuvenated and opens us to the possibilities for many peak experiences in the discovery along the way. As we are able to realize the childlike joy of a personal relationship to the game of golf, we establish the core values that mature into a far-reaching wisdom. Our connection in life to the sincere participation in all of the chosen endeavors opens us to a profound understanding of our ultimate capabilities. As we recognize self-actualized achievements in the game, the instinctive, unique qualities that we bring to our play allow for a creative participation that is always uninhibited and authentically original. This self-awareness continues to allow for the motivation and desire of the continued growth for which we strive. As we look back at each round that we play throughout our lives, we must realize that whatever the outcome, we played our game with a passion for the love of it. For in the end *it's* only a game—but what a game *it* really is. As each playing season passes, we look forward to the next as hope always springs eternal within the content of character. The cornerstone that we build our support system on provides the strength of commitment that slowly reveals the magical secrets that lie within the spirit of golf. When we are able to structure a purpose from the depths of passion, we are assured that the experience is personally ours. Conscious awareness will become clearly focused and opened to the full capacity of the courage and confidence encountered. The joy that we share as we overcome obstacles lies along the unique design in the course of play.

If the purpose remains true, our lives continue to unfold in a natural evolution. We are guided by the universal laws that attract us to what becomes necessary for continued forward momentum. Our mind-set then finds the peaceful acceptance of the challenges that we confront as we achieve a grateful, peaceful, serenity that secures our individual scared space. As we are more able to channel the force, the choices are defined not only from intellect, but also from our instinct. Goals and objectives are effortlessly accomplished and appreciated as our own doing and we are able to achieve maximum potential.

Now, the pursuits of golf and life are supported by a willingness to encounter ever changing circumstances that may, at times, divert us from what seems to be the way of our journey, only to reveal a better direction. If we remain open to a unique personal path and follow the guiding star of universal connection, all of our desires will become reality.

As I come now to the final words in this labor of love, the rising sun is shining through the door of my home. I sit here at my writing table while the golden, penetrating rays cast a shadow across my tablet, as if it were adding a final statement to what I have had the privilege of sharing. I wish for all of you, who have arrived at this point in my effort, to awaken a spark of creative enthusiasm that lies somewhere within your spirit.

Just as the sun continues to rise on your new day and illuminates the next opportunity to achieve a sense of well-being, allow yourself the freedom to *go fore it.*

Acknowledgments

A lifetime of experience and the realizations that have been captured in the completion of this book never would have occurred without the assistance of many people along the way. There are two in particular who have been most significant in the final completion of this project.

Jessica Ricco came into my life at the exact time when I needed the help that she was more than capable of providing. Her presence exemplifies the essence of the law of attraction. She has served as my web designer, photographer, editor, technical advisor, and friend. Her commitment to professionalism clearly demonstrates the "Going Fore It" attitude that compliments my pursuit. Without her the message transcribed never would have been completed with the clarity of its final form.

For my beloved wife, Beth, she is the one to whom this book is dedicated. If it were not for her unfailing devotion and belief in my mission, the determination required would have been more difficult to achieve. She has always been my greatest advocate. Our life together, both on and off the golf course, has provided the inspiration for much of the content in these pages. She is my soul mate, my best friend, and without a question my favorite golfing buddy. Our memorable moments spent together have instilled the passion and clarity of purpose. As together we endured the process, we have achieved the completion of the pursuit.

To the many students, both past and present, that I have had the privilege to have served. You have all supplied me with the insight that has structured the content of my efforts within these pages. I hope that you can take what I have shared and apply it to your lives in productive ways that bring out the best that you have to offer. The memories of your successes will be in my mind forever. Your commitment to the game is my reason for teaching. Remember always to practice with patience and perseverance.

To the game of golf, you have taught me so much about myself through the life force of our partnership. As a trusted friend and confidant your commitment to my growth and self-esteem has been unfailing. The challenges of your requirements have provided a passionate dedication to the values that carry me forward in life. The high ideals you represent have penetrated to the heart and soul of my being. I will always treasure your message and attempt to share it with as many others as possible.

My thanks to the game of golf for providing the capability and capacity to carry out this effort to completion. Getting to know your meaning has been the structural support for the cornerstone of passion that has inspired the support structure for this book. You have trusted me to share your message. I hope that it has been conveyed in the manner in which it was always intended.

Finally to my many acquaintances as you continue on the course of your life outside of the game of golf. What I have learned from you away from the course has solidified the relationship of life experiences as a reflection of the challenge that lies within my course of play.

Thank you to all,
Gil Anderson

Suggested Readings

1. The Seven Spiritual Laws of Success by Deepak Chopra, Quantum Publications

2. Beyond the Fairway by Jeff Wallach, Bantam Books

3. Your Sacred Self by Dr. Wayne W. Dyer, Harper Collins Publishers

4. Golf for Enlightenment by Deepak Chopra, Harmony Books

5. Golf in the Kingdom by Michael Murphy, Penguin Books

6. The Mulligan by Ken Blanchard & Wally Armstrong, Zondervan

7. Zen Golf by Joseph Parent, Doubleday

8. The Legend of Bagger Vance by Steven Pressfield, Avon Books

9. The Inner Game of Golf by W. Timothy Gallwey, Random House

10. Golfirmations by Hugh O'Neill, Rutledge Hill Press

11. Mind Over Golf by Dr. Richard Coop with Bill Fields, Macmillan Company

12. Freddie and Me by Tripp Bowden, Skyhorse Publishing

13. Zinger by Paul Azinger with Ken Abraham, Harper Collins

For more information on Gil's lessons, clinics, and speaking engagements please visit www.goingforeit.com or send an e-mail to gil@goingforeit. com.